DARK LIGHT
The John Witcombe Story

EILEEN E. LANTRY

Pacific Press Publishing Association
Boise, Idaho
Ottawa, Ontario, Canada

Edited by Bonnie Tyson-Flyn
Cover and inside design by Michelle C. Petz
Typset in 12/15 New Baskerville

Copyright ©1996 by
Pacific Press Publishing Association
Printed in the United States of America
All Rights Reserved

Library of Congress Cataloging-in-Publication Data:

Lantry, Eileen E., 1923-
   Dark light—the John Witcombe Story : He thought he was following new light—then God opened his eyes / Eileen E. Lantry.
     p. cm.
   ISBN 0-8163-1312-1 (pbk. : alk paper)
   1. Witcombe, John C. (John Charles), 1955- . 2. Seventh-day Adventists—United States—Biography. 3. Ex-cultists—United States—Biography. 4. Perfection—Religious aspects—Seventh-day Adventists. 5. Seventh-day Adventists—Doctrines. I. Lantry, Eileen E. II. Title.
BX6193.W56A3 1996
286.7'092—dc20
[B]   96-13413
                                                  CIP

Table of Contents

- 1 -
The Orange Juice
.... 5

- 2 -
I'll Do It My Way
.... 11

- 3 -
God Loves Rebels Too
.... 19

- 4 -
The Mask Came Off
.... 31

- 5 -
Do I Have a Blind Spot?
.... 39

- 6 -
A Man of Authority
.... 47

- 7 -
The Righteous Deceiver
.... 59

- 8 -
Me, Bring Unity?
.... 65

- 9 -
Can't Pin Me Down
.... 73

- 10 -
Separation
.... 81

- 11 -
The Victory-Now Message
.... 95

- 12 -
We Belong Nowhere
.... 101

- 13 -
I Will Make Darkness Light
.... 111

- 14 -
Discovered: Two Sides of Truth
.... 117

- 15 -
Epilogue
.... 127

This story of John and Sharon Witcombe's journey from darkness to light is written to help those who also may be sincerely confused. Never did the Witcombes lose their love for God. Even in their error, God did not forsake them. The reason we have shared their zeal and heartache is to proclaim God's great love and compassion for His children.

In order to protect the privacy of many of the people involved with the story, I have chosen to change names, to be vague in mentioning places and circumstances, and have omitted many situations that might be misunderstood or sound critical of the dear ones who have chosen to separate from the Seventh-day Adventist Church into independent ministries.

It is my prayer, together with John and Sharon, that this story may bring many of God's children back to a closer fellowship and relationship with God's remnant church, and together we may soon welcome the return of our loving, forgiving Lord.

The Orange Juice

I reached into the refrigerator and drew out a carton of orange juice. *This'll taste great!* I thought as I wiped the sweat off my face. About to perish from thirst after scrubbing down my RV during the hottest part of the afternoon, I felt so thirsty I didn't even bother to pour a glassful. Instead, I turned the carton up and took three big swallows. The golden liquid felt cool as it ran down my throat, and it tasted so-o-o-o . . . Then it hit me. Something was terribly wrong with the taste and the texture of that juice.

I glanced into the carton in my hand, and my stomach lurched. "Ugh, yuck!" I exclaimed, as I rushed toward the sink and retched. Floating on top of the orange juice was the most awful-looking green slime.

Suddenly, I couldn't stand being anywhere near that foul liquid. "Get out of here," I yelled. Dashing to the front door, I threw the carton out into the roadside.

Then I sat bolt upright in bed. "Get out of here!" I yelled again.

My wife, Sharon, grabbed my arm. "John, what's the matter?" she asked as she sat up beside me. "You're in bed. Who do you want to get out of here?"

I looked at her. The moonlight shining through the curtains revealed a worried look on her face. A lock of hair hung across the left side of her forehead. I put my hand over my eyes and shook my head. Reality returned gradually.

Sharon's arm slipped around my waist, and she snuggled up to me, but she didn't say anything. She just laid her head on my shoulder and patted my arm with her other hand.

Now wide awake, I felt my forehead. It was clammy. I could feel an inward shaking–my whole body quivered from an unknown dread.

"I guess I had a bad dream."

"Do you want to talk about it?" Sharon asked.

I opened my mouth to tell her, but the words stuck in my throat. A cold chill spread across my body, and my muscles tensed. Was the dream prophetic?

I could tell that Sharon felt the tension, because her hand tightened on my arm. "What is it, honey?" she asked again.

I lowered my face and rubbed my fingers across my forehead once more. "I . . . I . . . I can't talk about it now," I stammered. "Let's try to go back to sleep."

Sharon sighed and laid back down with her head on her pillow. A few minutes later, her slow, even breathing told me that she had gone back to sleep. I turned over and tried to

The Orange Juice

follow her example. The attempt was useless. Sleep evaded me the rest of the night, like clouds evade the sky over the Sahara. Was God trying to tell me something?

The horror of my nightmare didn't pass. As I stared into the darkness, an awful thought hit me. *John, your life is like that dream. Self-deception can twist your mind. What you think is pure could be polluted.*

Tossing and turning, I couldn't believe that a mind as sharp and clever as mine could be deceived. I shut my eyes and still seemed to taste the green slime. When I opened them, I glanced out the window and saw the first streaks of dawn. But inwardly, the darkness of midnight pressed hard. Was this strange nightmare from God or Satan? I sighed audibly, and this awakened Sharon.

"What's wrong, John?" she muttered, half asleep.

"That dream. I've been awake for hours. I can't shake off the dreadful feeling."

As she turned toward me, I extended my arm. She laid her head on my shoulder and snuggled close. For years we'd begun each day this way, praying together.

"Would you like to tell me about your dream first–or pray first?" And then she added, "I've never seen you so distraught."

"If I told you my dream, you could pray more intelligently."

A long minute passed before I could begin. I had just finished telling her the disgusting details when we heard footsteps and then a loud knock at the front door. We both knew who it was–our friends Karen and Irene, who had come to Germany with us from the United States. They were the last

DARK LIGHT

people I wanted to see right then, but I pushed aside my feelings and called, "Just a minute. I'll get my robe."

I wasn't prepared for what I saw when the door opened. In spite of the short distance between our RVs, they were both out of breath, their bathrobes skewed about their bodies like they'd thrown them on in a windstorm as they flew out the door. Fear was written all over their faces.

"What's wrong?" I asked.

"We have to talk." Irene, past sixty, spoke with a strong German accent.

"What about?" I asked.

I looked into her face for a clue, but all I could read was that she was dead serious about something. Even Karen, young and vivacious, looked solemn. I couldn't have been less prepared for Irene's answer. "I had a terrible dream last night. Haven't been able to sleep since then. Finally, I woke Karen and told her. We thought we ought to tell you."

My stomach lurched the way it had when I saw the green slime on the orange juice. I wasn't sure I wanted to hear her dream. In fact, I knew I didn't want to hear it, but I couldn't tell her to just go home. Finally, with a glance toward Sharon, who had just entered the room, I said as casually as I could, "Sit down and tell us about it."

They both sat down, and Irene took a deep breath. "Karen and I were driving our RV, following you and Sharon in yours. We were driving down the autobahn."

Karen interrupted, "You said we had just spent the past evening urging a group of people to get ready for the Lord to come."

"Yes, yes." Irene nodded her head vigorously. "Anyway,

The Orange Juice

before long, we came to a long tunnel. I can remember noticing the sunlight disappear on your motor home as you entered the tunnel. The next moment, we were both inside. We'd gotten halfway through the tunnel when the lights went out on my RV. I looked ahead and saw the lights go out on yours too. All was black darkness. Fortunately, there was no other traffic inside the tunnel either direction."

Irene paused. Her next words came out slowly, evenly, almost like she was thinking about each word as she spoke it. "John, we were totally in the dark!" She punctuated the word *dark* with her voice, then continued.

"We couldn't see any light at the end of the tunnel, either. Panic-stricken in the total darkness, I was afraid I'd hit you in the blackness. Grabbing my CB radio, I called frantically, 'We can't see our way to go forward.' Then I screamed, 'We must turn back now!' and the scream woke me up."

Irene leaned back in her chair, but she didn't relax. She kept her eyes on mine. I looked at the floor. Nobody said a word, and it seemed that I could feel the silence crawling over my skin.

"Well, what do you think?" Irene said at last.

I'd been dreading that question. "I don't know." I glanced over at Sharon. "But I think I need to tell you about a dream I had last night."

"You had a dream too?" Irene and Karen said the words together.

I told my dream–about coming in hot and sweaty from washing the RV, about reaching for the orange juice and

taking three huge swigs, and about how good I thought it tasted until I paused for a breath. Then I described how awful it looked and how I retched and gagged and threw the whole lot out the front door.

When I was through, we all sat back in our chairs and looked at each other. Except me–I looked at the floor. My eyes were focusing on a spot of dirt on the white kitchen tile. It seemed to have legs and a body, like a spider. Then I became aware that everyone else was looking at me. I looked from one to the other, but no one spoke. I knew they expected me to say something.

Finally, Karen broke the silence. "John, you're the leader of this group," she said. "What do you think?"

That question was the hardest one I'd ever faced in my life. The answer I feared tore the foundation out from under everything I'd done for the previous ten years. After another moment of silence I said, "Maybe God is trying to tell us something."

Again there was a long silence. Then Karen came up with the next obvious question–the one I knew we were all thinking but afraid to ask. "If God is trying to tell us something, what is it?" When I remained silent, she continued. "Could it be that all this time we've thought we were doing God's will, we've been blind and have been traveling down a crooked way in the wrong direction?"

Still unnerved by the vivid dream, I inwardly agreed with her. But my pride would not allow me to admit it. Attempting to sound confident, I countered, "If God has not been leading us over the years, why would He have answered so many of our prayers?"

I'll Do It My Way!

Finally, Irene and Karen left! I fled to the bathroom and took longer than usual to shave. When we sat down for a breakfast of hot cereal with soymilk and toast, our seven-year-old daughter, Traci, asked, "Where's the orange juice?" Sharon glanced at me and said, "Let's just drink milk this morning."

I followed her cue to change the subject with, "Please pass the peanut butter."

"I think I'll take a long walk down that dirt road." I pointed out the window as I swallowed the last bite of toast. "Might be relaxing to get a close look at Germany's beautiful countryside. Don't know just when I'll be back."

Sharon gave me a faint smile. "I understand, John."

With each step, Karen's words pounded into my brain. "John, you're the leader. What do you think?"

My thoughts whirled.

Leader! I love to lead. But am I a deceived leader? The blind leading the blind? Strong convictions I cherished had compelled me to plan this trip to Europe. I believed God had given me a special message for these last days. Wherever I shared my insights, many people accepted them. These many successes had reinforced my confidence in the Holy Spirit's leading. Should someone disagree, I smothered him or her with an avalanche of facts and quotations that refuted and silenced their objections. True, some poor souls rejected my logical presentations of truth. Pitying their lost condition, I followed Jesus' counsel. With vigor I shook the dust from my feet and left them lost in their error.

At that moment a disturbing text popped into my mind. Hadn't Paul suggested, "In honour preferring one another" (Romans 12:10)? I cringed. I knew my attitude didn't compare with the lowly Jesus. For the first time, I questioned the motives that had driven me to spend years in long hours of research and study. Was it to learn God's will–or to prove my rightness?

This morning in Germany, I couldn't shake this uneasiness, this nagging uncertainty, or these dreams. Though I stood six feet three, my foundation of values seemed to be reeling like an earthquake. Yes, I was a leader, but who had been leading *me*?

My thoughts raced backward to my early life. Perhaps I'd find some answers there. A seventh-generation Adventist, I grew up on a farm in Washington State. Dad and Mom repeatedly stressed, "You kids must learn the importance of work and responsibility. We expect you to help with your church-school tuition by working with the family chicken and egg business." During my first two years at Auburn Academy, I had worked on grounds and maintenance.

At the beginning of my junior year, I approached Dad. "I'm embarrassed to take my girlfriend out in that old '52 Plymouth. I've got my eyes on a '67 Pontiac GTO."

"Can you earn enough money to keep up the payments and the insurance? Remember, John, we expect top grades in your studies. I'll finance the old Plymouth, but nothing more."

"But, Dad, if I can get a job working on our neighbor's dairy farm, I think I could swing it. May I ask him?"

"He's a slave driver. He'll make you work long hours. That'll really cut into your school life."

"I'll continue to get A's and B's, I promise. Please, Dad, I want that car so much!"

"Think it through, John. You'll work each morning from two to six, then rush to school by seven. You know those three hundred cows must be milked twice a day, so your evenings are shot too. That's a terrible grind. You're sacrificing a lot for a fancy car."

Blind to his counsel, I chose not to listen. I wanted that car! Our neighbor knew my work habits and dependability. He hired me on the spot with these orders. "I'll expect you here every day but your Friday night and Sabbath. Besides milking, you're to feed the cows and calves, set out hay, and scrape and hose the barn."

Determined to show my dad I could own that car, I

agreed. In no time, I mastered the procedures and the milking machines. But the cows weren't inclined to cooperate. They'd swish me with their dirty, smelly tails; knock the machines from their udders; and kick me as I put the machine back in place. With twelve machines going at once, my frustration rose, and my temper flared. Alone in the milking barn, I vented my anger by calling the cows bad names and kicking them back. Every time I did it, I felt a twinge of guilt. I knew Jesus heard and saw me, even if no one else knew.

Anger soon became the norm. Too tired to care, I worked automatically, almost with my eyes closed. But I did feel ashamed. I couldn't quiet my conscience and admitted to myself that a growing Christian should try harder to develop self-control. I didn't like that angry part of me.

Keeping awake soon became a major problem. I never thought of asking God for help but solved the problem with my radio. From that time on, I worked with the blaring sound of rock music.

One evening I heard myself swear at a cow as I kicked it hard. I'd never cursed before, and I felt terrible. When I finished work, I ran out to the woods and sat on a log. Tears trickled down my cheeks as I cried, "Lord, I feel all mixed up. My life's becoming a mess. I just keep sinning, feeling guilty, and then asking You to forgive me. Isn't there some way to get victory?"

One day in Bible class, I found a text that described my life. "Now if I do what I will not to do, it is no longer I who do it, but sin that dwells in me" (Romans 7:20, NKJV).

I'll Do It My Way!

About this time, we kids convinced Mom and Dad that we needed a television set. "Just to watch nature programs and the news," we rationalized. Strange how quickly TV replaced family worships and how soon our parents relaxed their strict viewing rules. I remember developing the art of taking quick showers during commercials, afraid I'd miss something. But often, while milking alone in the barn, a voice in my brain suggested, *John, you'd be a misfit in heaven. You'd never be happy there. You're addicted to rock music and TV.*

One week I heard of a rock concert and dance to be held in a nearby town on Friday night. I puzzled a long time, trying to figure out a way to uphold my Sabbath-keeping standards and still enjoy the concert. As I milked cows on that Friday morning, my one-sided reasoning went like this: *It's wrong to buy and sell on the Sabbath, so I can't buy a ticket. I have no way to get one in advance. Since I can't do business on the Sabbath, I must find a way to sneak in without paying the fee.*

Not once did it occur to me that the command "Thou shalt not steal" was in the same ten as "Remember the Sabbath to keep it holy." I reasoned this way: *I don't go to movies with the other kids. Dancing is great exercise. I never touch drugs, alcohol, or tobacco. Every night I say my prayers. God knows I intend to be a Christian.*

Somehow I ended my junior year with a GPA of 4.0 in spite of the long hours at the dairy. So that I could take my girlfriend to the Saturday-night programs, I began to work Friday nights. Too tired to keep awake, I slept through church. Even though I wouldn't admit it to Dad,

I knew I had become a slave to owning my fancy car–and I had almost no time to enjoy it.

One Sunday morning, I woke up with a fever of 103 degrees. I called my employer. "I feel terrible. I'm too sick to come to work."

"Come anyway. The cows must be milked."

"But I can't. I have a high fever and ache all over."

"If you don't come," the farmer yelled, "I'll fire you."

"Then I'm through," I shouted back, and I slammed down the receiver.

Later, he apologized, urging me to return. "No. I've made my decision." Relieved, I sold my car, glad to work at the academy four hours a day for lower wages.

One Sabbath morning during my senior year, I happened to listen to the sermon. I picked up on something that sounded like the solution to my problem of lousy attitudes and lifestyle. The preacher quoted, "Sanctification is the work of a lifetime."

That's it! I thought. *God doesn't expect a young person to have it all together yet. Someday I'll conquer my temper and give up rock. Nothing to worry about now. I've got a lifetime ahead to grow like Christ. No need to worry now about reaching the goal of sanctification.*

Wow! Such a simple, quick solution to the problem that had bugged me so long! Why hadn't I thought of this before?

But I blocked out the minister's next words. "Sanctification is like eating. To maintain physical life, you must spend a lifetime eating. It's the same with sanctification. Every day of your life, Christ must live in you anew. Jesus

I'll Do It My Way!

planned for you to continue to eat to maintain physical life. To have a successful Christian life, you must also live daily by His power. It is not a goal to be reached. It is a life to be lived."

I didn't agree. My mind was as sharp as his. Satisfied with my "right" conclusion, I closed my mind and settled the problem. If it took a lifetime to grow up like Christ, I could wait. What a relief!

With my religious problem solved, I concentrated on graduating with top grades, having fun, and planning for college. Yet I couldn't shake off that vague fear that I'd become a slave to TV, rock, and my trigger temper.

At Walla Walla College, my standards took another nose dive when I joined the guys who sneaked out to see movies. One evening, I slipped out of the dorm for a walk. "Tonight, I'm making a decision," I said aloud. "I hate feeling horrible, mixed-up, uncomfortable. It's either one lifestyle or the other. I know I'm sliding downhill spiritually—and fast! So what? All around me I see hypocrites–kids who claim to be Christians but whose lives don't show it!"

After an hour of walking, I stopped. The lights of the college were far away. I looked toward the stars and shouted defiantly, "Christianity doesn't work! It's nothing but a joke! I'm tired of living with this sin/defeat syndrome! I'm going to quit trying! Throw it all out! I'm going to start down a different path!"

Having made my decision, I turned back toward the dormitory. As I walked, I began to formulate a plan for a new life and new goals–a life without Christ.

First, I need a girlfriend, definitely not the Christian type. One who "knows the ropes," who looks and acts like she's been around in the world. She can show me how to live it up!

Always a "now" person, I began my search. This one goal consumed my thinking. I looked constantly. On campus, in the halls, at the dining room, in class, yes, even at church. Then I spotted her. Slender, pretty, hair my color of brown, cute, flippant manner. She wore her makeup well and had an attitude of glamour and worldliness.

I watched her for several days. *She's the one! About five feet seven, just right for me. I must find out her name.*

But when I discovered that Sharon was a sophomore, I was dismayed. Would she date an eighteen-year-old freshman?

God Loves Rebels Too

That evening during study period, I called Sharon. My heart beat wildly as I waited for her to come to the phone. Then I heard, "Hello, this is Sharon."

"And this is John Witcombe. We haven't met, but I'd like to get acquainted with you. Will you go with me to the concert?"

There was a long pause. Then she spoke slowly. "Sorry. I have other plans."

"Thanks anyway." I tried to sound nonchalant. "I'll contact you again."

Feeling dejected, I pondered the brushoff. *Do I dare try again?*

Each day, I looked for Sharon and tried to be where she was, but somehow she always slipped away before we could speak. Once I caught her looking at me, but when

our eyes met, she turned away.

I called again the following week.

"Sorry. I have a date with someone else." Her tone of voice sounded different, as if she really did feel sorry. A few days later, she went out of her way to meet me on the sidewalk. When she smiled and said "Hi," my heart did a flip-flop. We chatted briefly before she left.

The next day, I played table tennis with her roommate's boyfriend. He played a good game, but this time I beat him. When we stopped to rest, he said, "Let's cool off in the pool. I think my girlfriend is there. Want to join us?"

"Sure, let's head for the locker room," I answered.

Before we dived into the pool, Sharon's roommate stopped by the phone. After she dialed, I heard her say, "Hi, Sharon. We're at the pool. Want to come swimming?" A long pause.

"Oh, it's only eight-thirty, not bedtime yet. Besides, it might interest you to know that John Witcombe is here with us." Another pause, but shorter.

"OK. We'll see you in a few minutes."

Soon Sharon joined us at the swimming pool. Thoughtfully the roommate and her boyfriend left us alone so we could get acquainted. I couldn't believe time could go so fast. We talked till almost ten. As we walked back to the dormitory, I wanted to hold her hand but felt I didn't dare. Just before we said good night, I asked, "May I take you to the international dinner next week?"

She looked up at me in amazement; then her eyes began to smile. "Yes," she answered, "I'll go with you."

The rest of the week, I lived in the joy of anticipation. I

planned what I'd say to her. Would she understand my longing for freedom from all the miserable restrictions of religion? How exciting life could be with this dream girl! Already I felt confident that she'd make it easy to change my focus on life and forget God. No more church rules. With her, I could enjoy a world of fun.

Sitting across from her at the international dinner, I thought, *She's the most beautiful girl I've ever seen.* When we finished the meal, we pushed our chairs over into a corner. I began my planned speech.

"Sharon, up to now, I'd say my religious life has been a mess filled with failures. If God gave out grades, I'd rate a D-minus on my lousy attempts to live the Christian life. I've discovered that Christianity just doesn't work for me. I don't know anyone who lives what the Bible teaches. Frankly, I've decided to throw it all out, and . . ."

But Sharon interrupted me. "You too, John? Talk about messes and failures, I can top them all. And I'm sick of it. My life seems empty, pointless, self-centered, full of dumb decisions."

"But you act so carefree," I objected, "like you're having a great time. Aren't you happy?"

I remember the tingling of disappointment that ran through me when I saw the hurt look on her face. "Far from it, John. I hate my kind of fun. It doesn't last. Most of the time, I'm plagued with guilt and remorse, hurting inside."

My heart sank. *Is there a different Sharon inside? Has she been wearing a worldly mask? If so, I like it. Is she about to blast my hopes and plans?*

DARK LIGHT

"But, Sharon, I don't understand," I objected. "I like you just the way you are."

"That's because you don't know me, John. Would you like to hear a little about my life?."

I wanted to, and I didn't want to. Yet, snared by her charm, I couldn't say No. Before I could answer, she added, as if weighing her thoughts carefully, "We hardly know each other, John, but there's something about you that makes me feel I can be honest with you and open up my heart."

Half scared yet terribly curious, I consented. "Let's go sit in the lobby so we can talk without interruption."

Once we were settled in the lobby, Sharon began, "I grew up an Adventist. We lived all over the U.S. My dad was a church-school teacher, and we moved frequently. Through high school, I complied with my folks' strict standards, though I'll admit I stretched them to the limits, like wearing my skirts as short as I dared. After graduation, my parents suggested that I learn to be a medical missionary at a self-supporting facility in Colorado.

"I refused and begged to go to Pacific Union College, where my friends would be attending.

"But the more I thought about it, the more the adventure appealed to me. It might be fun to see if I could cope with their unique lifestyle. I was challenged to see if I could play their game for a while and succeed."

"How'd you manage?" I asked.

"At first, I wore my mask well. The girl with a happy, submissive attitude. Seeing my cooperation, the staff trusted me. Their rules made sense, though I had a struggle wearing dresses halfway between my knees and ankles. I got good grades in my classes, even found the healthful food quite tolerable.

"But as the months went by, I grew tired of 'playing good.' It was so lonely. I didn't fit into their mold; I wasn't on their wavelength. Eventually, my 'righteous veneer' began to wear thin. From my body language, my attitudes—whatever—they detected my insincerity.

"Soon I detected ways in which the staff tried to convert me. Friday-evening meetings became unbearable. It seemed that each speaker looked straight at me and pleaded, 'Please come and give your life to Jesus.' Drenched in horrible guilt, I sat in awful, oppressive silence, stubbornly resisting each invitation.

I hate this! I thought. *They're forcing me to become a Christian.* But another thought hit me, *No, it's Jesus. He's calling you, not these people.*

"I wanted to flee from this oppressive atmosphere, so I began taking long walks in the surrounding hills. Carefully I hid my transistor radio under my sweater, hoping I'd meet that nice guy who sat near me in class. I walked the direction the boys usually walked, hiking among the pine trees to the sound of rock music."

"So who's your favorite rock group?" I interrupted.

Sharon refused to change the subject and went on. "One time I did meet that guy in a wooded area. 'Hello there,' he called. 'What are you doing here?'

"My heart pounded so fast I could hardly breathe. *What if we get caught?* I felt bashful and couldn't think of anything to say. Finally, I gasped out an embarrassed Hi,

DARK LIGHT

turned, and almost ran the other way.

"After one terribly long Friday-evening altar call, I decided I couldn't endure church the next morning. Very early I sneaked out, intending to hike the ten miles to town. I'd walked only a short distance when a car stopped. The driver called, 'Want a ride?'

"He left me by a lake. I sat on a bench watching the boats, when a young man approached me.

'How about doing a bit of waterskiing?'

'I'm not very good at it,' I answered.

'Then maybe you'd drive my boat while I ski?'

'If you'll teach me what to do.' I felt a twinge of conscience but stifled it with the thought, *I'm not a Christian, so why try to keep the Sabbath? I might as well enjoy myself.*

"As I hitchhiked back that evening, I thought, *I've not had this much fun for months. Lots better than the boring Sabbaths I've endured.*

"The next morning, five months after I'd arrived, the staff called me in. 'Sharon, your rebellious attitude has convinced us that it is best for you to leave right away.'

"Relieved, I complied. Finished with hypocritical 'righteousness,' I returned home."

"And how did your parents react?" I asked.

"I'm ashamed to tell you, John, that everything about me reeked with rebellion and bitterness. I made home a place of constant conflict. Insisting on my own way, I showed my defiance with the shortest miniskirts I could find, plenty of makeup and jewelry, and late-night dates with boys of low standards. My lifestyle plummeted to match theirs. My former shyness vanished after a few drinks at the wild parties.

"The situation worsened. Finally, my mother laid down the law. 'Sharon, we cannot allow you to keep company with these boys!'

" 'Then I'm leaving home. My boyfriend will be happy to have me stay with him.' And I did leave. I tried most of the 'taboo' things, but I didn't like alcohol, drugs, and tobacco. Guess they conflicted with my former healthful tastes. Fortunately, I never formed these hard-to-break habits."

"You're lucky, Sharon," I said. "But how come you're here at Walla Walla?"

"My boyfriend and I moved to California, where he enrolled in Stanford University. I was left alone every day in the apartment. I finally figured out that I was wasting my time, so I decided to come here and begin my freshman year. But my lifestyle didn't change. Every day after classes, I hitchhiked to town with kids like me. My non-Christian roommate was kicked out when she became pregnant. My next roommate had no interest in God and secretly smoked. Spiritually, my freshman year was a disaster. At the end of the school year, I received a letter from my Aunt Carol, who lived in Washington, D.C., inviting me to spend the summer with them. My parents consented, and Dan, my favorite cousin, was going too. They actually seemed to want me to come.

"*Great*, I thought. *So Mom and Dad don't enjoy fighting any more than I do. I can be free to do as I want in that big city. Dan and I can really live it up!*

"Aunt Carol accepted me just as I was, though I felt

guilty about the terrible example I set for her daughter. Every time Dan and I went sightseeing, we'd stop for a drink–though neither of us liked alcohol. One weekend, I skipped out with a guy my aunt knew had a bad reputation. When I was far from the city, I called her. 'Just wanted you to know I'm safe, so don't worry. I'll be home Sunday night.'

" 'I'll be praying for you. Thanks for calling,' was all she said.

"I had reason to be glad for those prayers. The two of us went to a state park and hiked to the top of a high waterfall. While I was leaning over the edge to look down at the hundred-foot drop, my foot went out from under me. I heard my boyfriend gasp, but he couldn't catch me. I fell backward and somehow grabbed onto a bush, which saved me from certain death.

"Back home I wondered, *Why didn't I die? Why doesn't my aunt preach or push her ideas on me?*

"I found my answer by eavesdropping while Aunt Carol talked with a friend. 'Words can't describe my inner peace. These past months, I've discovered a new relationship with Jesus.' Aunt Carol then explained to her friend that even though she had been a Christian all her life, she'd never before known such joy, such freedom from guilt and sin. Through months of prayer and study on righteousness by faith in Him, she experienced the joy of victory.

"John, I didn't know what peace was. Always I've been fiercely independent; I wouldn't give in to anyone. What she said gave me a glimmer of hope.

"One day when we were alone in the house, I asked, 'Aunt Carol, I heard you telling your friend of an exciting experience you're having with Jesus. You know what a rebellious rascal I am. Do you think I could ever know that kind of peace and joy?'

"I'll never forget her words as she hugged me. 'If you ever want to become a Christian and really mean business with God, don't begin by trying to give up your bad habits. Instead, just start reading of Jesus' life. Let Him fill you full of His power and love. When you fall in love with Jesus, everything else will come into focus.' "

Sharon paused. Her words brought memories I wanted to bury. My expression must have given me away, for she asked, "Am I making you uncomfortable, John?"

"A little," I admitted.

"Shall I stop?"

Part of me didn't want to hear anymore. I didn't like the trend of her story. But my desire to understand this charming girl won. "No, go on," I said.

"OK." She smiled that special way I liked and continued. "Toward the close of last summer, another aunt and uncle came to visit Aunt Carol. 'We're driving to Idaho to see your folks. We'd like to take you home, Sharon. No expense to you.'

"I fell asleep somewhere in Colorado. When the car stopped, I woke up to the words 'Let's stop here for the night.' Horror swept over me as I recognized the brick buildings–it was the same medical missionary training school where I'd previously felt incarcerated. All the unpleasant pressures of those Friday-evening meetings

rolled onto me. I couldn't stay there overnight. As soon as they went into the building, I slipped away. Wearing only jeans and a halter top–and with very little money in my pocket–I ran to the highway, hoping I'd be picked up soon."

"You mean a pretty girl like you decided to hitchhike all the way home alone?" I asked incredulously.

"Uh-huh. I told you I've made a lot of stupid decisions. The first truck driver took me a long distance, and he treated me respectfully. But when the second driver picked me up, I sensed danger. As he started making advances, I pushed him away. He reached over again. 'Stop!' I yelled. 'You bet I'll stop, and we'll have fun!' He sneered as he turned off the freeway to a side street in a small town. As he slowed to turn a corner, I flung open the door and jumped out. Fortunately, people nearby came running toward me when I fell, so he drove away. Now I know God saved me from what could have been tragedy."

I shuddered at what might have happened but said nothing. Sharon continued, "I rode with the third driver until long after dark. With unusual consideration for my safety, he said, 'I live in the next city, but I can't take you home. My wife wouldn't like that. I'm going to take you to a hostel where the "Jesus-hippies" stay. You'll be safe there.'

"A group of long-haired kids sat studying their Bibles. I had no desire to join them, so I went to bed. The next day, another truck driver offered me a ride. God must love rebels, for this guy also cared more about my safety than about sex. 'I'm going all the way to Idaho. You look tired,' he said, 'Crawl up into the sleeping compartment while I drive.' Don't you think, John, that God sends angels in spite of our dumb decisions?"

I didn't want to comment, for I knew I was a rebel too. Sharon took the cue and kept on with her story.

"My folks were glad to send me back to college for my sophomore year. Here I was–lonely, depressed, wretched, overwhelmed with my empty, pointless life. Hangovers from wild parties seemed better than the crushing ugliness and guilt of sin. I had no true friends, not even a boyfriend to confide in. Then I remembered my aunt's words. Why not try God? Alone in my room, I picked up a book my parents had given me long ago, *The Desire of Ages*. Each chapter included a list of Scripture references from the Gospels.

"*I'll give it a try*, I thought. I remembered another suggestion my aunt had given me. 'You'll be greatly blessed if you ask first for the Holy Spirit to help you.' I was out of practice when it came to prayer, but I blurted out: 'OK, God. Here I am. I've ignored You for a long time. Been going down a really crooked path in the dark. But I have a feeling that You haven't forgotten me. Could You straighten out my life and give me peace? I think I'd like to know You better. Thanks a lot. Amen.'

"John, I've been enjoying Jesus for several weeks now. You may think this sounds silly, but I seem to see light in the darkness and feel like He's holding my hand. It's a strange, new joy. Maybe it's peace. I don't know which it is–but I love it. I'm actually eager for these special times with Jesus. Better than partying with my friends. John,

don't you think this is great?

By now, the evening program had ended, and couples walked passed us. I stood and turned toward the door so Sharon couldn't see my face. I had no desire to answer her question. I just wanted to escape.

"Sharon, I'm afraid it's time for me to take you back to the dorm. Let's continue this later," I said.

The Mask Came Off

Two days passed. Though I missed seeing Sharon, I needed time to evaluate all she had told me. Obviously, she wouldn't fit into my plans. I wanted the world, not God. Yet I felt drawn to Sharon. That afternoon, I went to the student center; I needed a quiet spot to be alone and think."

As I opened the door, I met her coming out. "Hi, John." She smiled and asked, "Are we still friends since you know so much about me?"

"Of course. But I'll admit you toppled my plans." I noticed she carried her Bible. "So you're still reading that Book about your new Friend."

"I really like Him, John, more all the time. Could we chat a few minutes?" We sat in two lounge chairs facing each other, and I could sense her excitement. Then sud-

denly she looked shy.

"I guess I've never shared my feelings with anyone like I did with you the other evening. But, John, I've felt so dirty for so long. Now I want to be clean—from the inside. I'm sure Jesus can make me a new person. Even give me the power to live like He did. I feel like I've been blind, and He's helping me see clearly so I won't make such dumb decisions."

I watched her eyes sparkle. "John, it's great getting to know Him. For the first time, I've felt joy and peace–the sweetest experience I've ever had!"

I tried not to show my disappointment, but she read it on my face. Nothing was going right. This wasn't what I wanted from Sharon. She pleaded, "John, His powerful love is drawing me. I'm falling in love with Jesus. Please, won't you listen to what my aunt told me?"

I looked at the floor. *Has the glitter I saw in the world only covered garbage? Do I want the "nothingness" of a life without God that Sharon experienced?* Suddenly, my decision to throw Christ out of my life and make a stab at the world seemed pretty dumb. But my pride stopped me from reconsidering.

"I'm not ready yet." I stood up and held out my hand. "Let's go get a malt." We saw each other several times the next week, but neither of us mentioned the one subject we were both thinking about.

One day, a smiling Sharon met me with a letter in her hand. "Just listen to this! My Aunt Carol is going to Canada to see her father. On the way, she plans to stop here in Walla Walla. Could God have arranged that trip,

The Mask Came Off

John, so you could listen to what she shared with me?"

Me, listen to what some old woman thinks? Yet I couldn't refuse Sharon's enthusiasm. I decided that I'd tell her aunt all the bad news of my life. That would cut the dreaded visit short.

The day her aunt arrived, Sharon phoned me. "Can you meet us in the dorm lobby?" she asked.

I'll make this short and quick. As soon as the introduction was over, I blurted out, "I think you should know that I'm through trying to be a Christian. I'm sick of this ugly merry-go-round–getting angry, feeling guilty, asking for forgiveness, feeling temporary relief, and getting angry again. I quit! Besides, I hate the restrictions. I'm fed up with compromises and guilt trips. The struggle to be good isn't worth the effort. I'm finished!"

Instead of being shocked, Aunt Carol smiled sympathetically. "I understand your problem, for I've been where you are. The reason that Christianity has never worked for you, John, is that you've never been a Christian."

Her statement struck me like a bolt of lightning. "What! You mean I've never been one! That this lousy life I see in myself and most everyone else isn't Christianity at all? Wow! that's good news!"

"The Bible describes the Christian life like this," she continued. " 'Thanks be to God, who gives us the victory through our Lord Jesus Christ' [1 Corinthians 15:57, NKJV]. Does that sound like your life?"

"Absolutely not! And it's the same for all the Christians I've known. An up-and-down experience. Like I said, sin, defeat, guilt, and then crawling to God to get forgiven. No real victories. Nobody can win this fight with Satan."

"Right, John, not with Satan. You can't overcome Satan, but Jesus can and has already done so. No wonder you're tired and want to quit. You've been fighting the wrong battle. If you fight the fight of faith through Jesus, you'll see victory."

"What!" I shook my head. "This victory you talk about can't be that easy. Most of the guys think I'm a pretty good fellow. Instead, I've been living a lie. Now I've given up. Don't tell me that for eighteen years I've been putting my efforts into fighting a useless battle! Is there a different set of rules in fighting this victory game? Is there hope for me?"

Aunt Carol smiled. "There's lots of hope, John. You've already admitted defeat. That's the first step. Now let God fight for you. When you give Him permission to take over, He'll give you the power to do His will. Then you're living by faith in Him. I promise you, He alone gives freedom from the power of sin."

I remembered the many times I'd lain awake for hours at night filled with a terrible fear of being lost–a life without God. My heart began to pound in excitement. "This last week, I've had second thoughts about throwing Christ completely out of my life. Yet the only way I knew to get rid of guilt was to get rid of God. Are you sure He's able to give me the power to overcome sin and be saved?"

"Yes, John, if you'll accept the promise 'I can do all things through Christ who strengthens me.' Jesus says, 'Ask, and it shall be given to you.' If you really mean it, I'd like to invite you to surrender to Him. Just give up; quit trying to overcome your sins by yourself. Give your entire life to God. That gives Him the right to give you His power. When He takes control, He gives you victory over your sinful desires and bad habits."

Could I really believe what she said? For the first time in my life, I admitted my helplessness. So I'd been self-deceived into thinking I could handle my life by my strong willpower. It made sense to give up and let Someone stronger than I take over. If God really wanted to take charge of my messed-up life, why not let Him?

I looked at Sharon's radiant face. God was changing her. Why not let Him do it for me? *Give up, John. Let go.* Always a now person, I answered, "Sounds good. I'd like to submit to His power and let Him take control of the whole mess."

Aunt Carol smiled. "God has been ready for a long time. Now that you are ready, too, why don't we step into the chapel and ask Him to take charge." Sharon and I knelt beside Aunt Carol. We each prayed a simple prayer giving God our all. Though my faith was small, I believed God would keep His promise. After Aunt Carol left, I didn't feel any different–but I knew I was.

The next day after classes, I went back to my room but stopped short in the doorway. The posters of seductive women covering the walls glared at me. *Sorry, Jesus. Guess these don't belong here anymore. I'm sure You don't like porn.* I ripped the posters off the wall. With them in one hand and a stack of cassettes in the other, I headed for the trash can.

On the way to the trash, a friend stopped me and asked, "Why are you throwing those cassettes away? Don't you like them anymore?"

"Yea, I like them–yet I don't." I could hardly believe the miracle that had taken place in my life. "I'm sort of like a recovering alcoholic. He always likes the stuff, but he chooses not to drink. Yesterday I asked God to take over in my life. He's done it! Before, rock controlled me. Now God's power turns me away from what I choose not to cultivate. Wow, what a God!"

My friend just shook his head and walked away.

I could hardly wait to tell Sharon. "Listen to this! It's a miracle. God helped me make a decision and stick to it. Since I invited Him to live in me, rock's gotta go. That's victory! Think of it, Sharon. This must be the fight of faith your aunt talked about. It's great stuff!"

"Neat sermon, John." Sharon smiled. "Ever thought of being a preacher?"

"Never. The last time I got up front–at my eighth-grade graduation–I forgot everything I'd planned to say. That one humiliation is enough to last a lifetime. But let me show you what I found in the lobby."

I handed her a small brochure advertising a self-supporting medical missionary facility in the South. "They're inviting people to go there to learn to become medical evangelists. Sounds interesting."

Sharon looked dubious. "Remember, I spent five months at a similar place a couple years ago. You'd find it difficult. Strict rules, unbending discipline. No association between the sexes either. Don't think you'd fit in very well."

The Mask Came Off

But the more I studied the Bible and the Spirit of Prophecy, the more convinced I became that this was the type of training God was calling me to take. Then the idea struck me. *I'll never last at that medical missionary school if I go there alone. But if I were married, it would be easier to tolerate the restrictions.* Yet I'd only known Sharon for a month. I decided to drop a strong hint and watch her reaction. If favorable, I'd pursue it further.

So on our next date I said, "Sharon, I'm really interested in learning to be a medical missionary. But I'm sure I couldn't live by their strict rules unless I was married."

Sharon smiled but said nothing. Was she happy to know that I was serious about both God and her?

Back in the men's dormitory, I joined a group of guys.

"Come down off cloud nine, John. Seems like we see you with Sharon most of the time," one fellow spoke up. "You couldn't be thinking of marriage?"

Foolishly, I spoke my thoughts. "I've never met a girl like her. Can't think of anyone I'd rather marry!"

That's all it took for the guys to assume that we were engaged. "Hear that, fellas. We've got a duty to perform. To the fish pond, John. That's what we do to all newly engaged men."

I protested loudly, "I'm not engaged. Stop! Stop!" But I struggled in vain. Fifteen guys grabbed me and threw me into the pond. The news got around quickly. That same evening, Sharon received a red rose in the women's chapel, another custom for newly engaged young woman.

I felt embarrassed when I met Sharon in the hall the next morning. "I didn't say we were engaged. The guys

assumed it. But," I hesitated, "it's a good idea. I feel like I already belong to you."

Sharon smiled as I squeezed her hand. We set no definite date, but both of us knew that someday we'd be together for life. For the present, getting to know Jesus had highest priorities for both of us.

Do I Have a Blind Spot?

Whenever possible, Sharon and I met together at the student center to study our Bibles, read from the Spirit of Prophecy, or just talk. Often we prayed together. God was drawing us closer to Him and to each other.

I developed a deep concern over the lowering of standards I saw on our campus. This grew to gigantic proportions the day I went to the college bindery on an errand. "Look here, John." A friend pointed to a stack of bound magazines. I read the title. My friend continued, "My boss said nothing when I told him it's not right for a Christian college to contract to bind pornography."

Immediately indignant, I decided, *I'm going to report this to the president. When he finds out, he'll do something about it.* But I didn't pray or seek counsel from God. No, I did as I had always done–tackle the problem my own way.

DARK LIGHT

In strong language, I described the situation to the president, asking, "How can you permit such wickedness to exist in a Christian college?" He definitely didn't appreciate my counsel but stood and escorted me to the door with no promise to follow my suggestions.

Now I decided that as a born-again Christian I must speak out against any lowering of standards. Hadn't I read in Ezekiel that we should "sigh and cry" about these abominations?

Like Nehemiah of old, I was a man of action. But I didn't copy his tactful methodology, nor did I ask God for guidance. No, I knew what to do. At the library, I discovered several pointed quotations from the *Index to the Writings of Ellen G. White* stating that Adventist institutions should refuse to bind or print any questionable materials. These gave real punch to the stinging article I wrote for the college paper entitled "College Bindery Indited."

Writing that article began my self-appointed quest to shock people from their lethargy. I felt called to point out the obvious inconsistencies at the college in order to begin a reformation. It seemed that every time I read the Bible or the Spirit of Prophecy, I found quotations that reinforced my agenda.

When the guys ribbed me with "Lay off, rabble rouser John," I thought, *Blessed are they that are persecuted for righteousness' sake*, and blindly pressed on.

Halfway through the second semester, I received a note that the vice-president wanted to see me. *Good,* I thought, *he's noticed my efforts to bring about a reformation. He probably wants to commend me for holding up the standards.*

Do I Have a Blind Spot?

When he asked me how school was going, I talked at length about my newly found joy in Jesus.

He listened, but when I paused, he looked very serious and said, "John, a few days ago, the monitor saw you sit in your roommate's seat, turn in his ticket, and then go to your own chapel seat and turn in your ticket. Is this compatible with Bible principles of honesty?"

My face turned red. "I didn't think that such a small thing was commandment breaking," I stammered as my self-righteous balloon popped.

Again and again, God began to pull back the curtain. Was He trying to open my blind eyes? Strange how hard it was to see my inconsistency surfacing here and there. While doing custodial work a few weeks earlier, I had found the answers to my psychology test on the teacher's desk. Great! I got an "A" without cracking the book. Now I had to go and confess to the professor that I'd cheated. I also had rounded off the hours on my time sheet all year, which meant I got paid for many hours I didn't work. It was tough for this "holier-than-thou" Christian to make that right with my boss.

Then one day in the cafeteria, my conscience shouted, *You're a thief–you've been stealing all year. Every day, you slip lunch meats under your plate in the cafeteria so the checker won't see.* I really felt cheap when I asked her to estimate the cost and add that to my bill.

Yet God showed me the same mercy He did those workers in the parable who arrived at the job site right before quitting time. He gave me the same generous supply of grace as those who beat the morning whistle.

When the school year ended, I returned home to Washington and Sharon, to Idaho. We had made no definite wedding plans.

Near my home, I found a job milking six hundred cows a day. Included in the wages was a small furnished house. Now I could begin to pay my school bills and get more reliable wheels than my Honda 350. By working long hours, I earned enough to keep up the payments on a good used pickup, pay my expenses, and save a little.

But my thoughts were of Sharon. After several weeks of eating tiresome meals of canned vegetables, I called her. "Honey, life is so empty without you. I'm terribly lonesome. I've got a good-paying job and a reliable pickup. I'd love to share this little house with you. I don't have much to offer, but would you consider setting our wedding date for sometime in August?"

And so I acquired the most beautiful bride in all the world on our special day–August 18, 1974.

After a short honeymoon in the mountains of British Columbia, we began life together at our little home at the dairy. But after a few weeks, Sharon said, "John, I love just keeping house for you, but we have school bills to pay. There's a job at a bakery in Auburn. Mind if I apply?"

"If you wish, but I'm afraid the hours of our jobs won't coincide. We'll not be home at the same time."

Several months went by. One evening, I declared, "We didn't get married to live apart. We seldom even get to eat together. I don't like this. Let's try to find something we can do together."

"Maybe we could become literature evangelists. I've

Do I Have a Blind Spot?

never sold books, but we could learn," Sharon suggested.

We started in Seattle. My persuasive talents gained a few sales, but we felt so sorry for the people who couldn't afford the books that we gave many of them away. After three unsuccessful months, we ran out of both money and food.

"Let's get a paper and look for some other kind of work," I suggested. That night, we studied the ads.

"Look here," Sharon read. "Wanted. Security guards for the Seattle Art Museum. If we could work together, that would be great. Let's apply tomorrow."

The next two-and-a-half years proved to be a continual honeymoon. What fun! We did everything together, both at work and at home. Best of all, we began growing up in Christ through hours spent in Bible study.

One evening, I suggested, "Let's study righteousness by faith. I'm not sure I agree with what our Sabbath School teacher said last week."

"Was the teacher right when he said that when Christ justified us at the cross, all our past sins were forgiven, and we're qualified for heaven?" Sharon asked.

"Yes, but didn't he imply that since Jesus made salvation sure on the cross, our works amount to nothing? I'm not comfortable with the implication that we now have freedom to do as we please. Surely there's a balance between faith and works."

"John, remember that text we read for worship this morning. I think it was Hebrews 13:21. "God says He works in us to do that which is pleasing in His sight, not ours. That doesn't agree with the teacher's comment that

legalistic vegetarians can now feel free to order a steak when they go out to eat."

The next Sabbath, we came home from church even more confused. Something seemed wrong with this theology. We spent all our free time for several months in study.

"I think I understand, Sharon," I said one evening. "We know Jesus' righteousness cannot cover sin. So every time we fall into sin–even a small, unintentional one, such as impatience or an unkind word–we're no longer justified. Until we ask forgiveness, we're in a lost condition."

Sharon shook her head. "I don't know, John. Something about that concept doesn't sound right to me. It seems like your focus would be on yourself instead of Christ. I'd get very discouraged if I thought I was lost and needed to be reconverted every time I slipped and fell."

"Listen, Sharon, you don't have to stay unjustified," I countered. "In a second, you can repent and ask forgiveness–and you'll be covered again. Not only that, I also believe that when we are justified, we won't be slipping into the same old sins again and again. I don't know why in the world you think my focus would be on myself. It's only God who can give victory to keep me from falling into sin."

I could see Sharon wasn't convinced. Was she stubborn—or was I?

"You may be right, John, but I doubt it. I know it's important to ask forgiveness when I've sinned, but I don't see why I need to believe I'm lost."

"But, Sharon, if people think that they are justified

Do I Have a Blind Spot?

while they are still sinning, they'll never stop. They must understand that true Christians don't sin. If they do, it's because they've lost their experience. They're not converted again until they repent. How can you possibly get around this quote?" I opened a red book and started reading.

> While God can be just, and yet justify the sinner through the merits of Christ, no man can cover his soul with the garments of Christ's righteousness while practicing known sins, or neglecting known duties. God requires the entire surrender of the heart, before justification can take place; and in order for man to retain justification, *there must be continual obedience*, through active, living faith that works by love and purifies the soul (*Selected Messages*, 1:366).

Sharon sighed. "John, you always win in our theological discussions. How can I argue with a quote?" She started to leave the room, but stopped abruptly.

"You might come to a different conclusion if you'd prayerfully consider the entire context of the source of your quotes."

Like a jackhammer, questions pounded my brain. *I know I amass quotations to prove a point. Is there a fine line between truth and error? Am I leading Sharon into error, blinded by my ideas on righteousness by faith? Can this be subtle error toward crooked paths that will affect our future?*

A Man of Authority

"Working in this art museum has become boring," Sharon commented. "All our bills are paid, and we've got money in our savings account. Don't you think we're ready for a new challenge?"

"I agree. How about going to that self-supporting medical missionary institute?"

"Seems like a great way to prepare to serve God," Sharon answered.

"Then I'll write and see if they have work for us."

So in the summer of 1977, we packed our things and headed for the South.

"I like this country of low hills and ridges. Great for hiking. According to the directions, we should be there in a few miles. Keep watching." I felt a sense of excitement.

Sharon sat on the edge of her seat. "There's the sign,

John. Are you ready for a new adventure?"

I turned in at the gate. We stopped the car and looked around. "That large building with pine trees around it must be the health center." Sharon pointed to the left. "Look at the small mobile homes. Not very fancy. Wonder if that's what we'll live in? But we'll make do. Somebody's doing a good job of caring for the grounds."

We went to the business office first. The business manager was apologetic. "We're short of homes, so families have to share a house." Eager to fit in, we accepted the cramped living quarters. We tried not to complain about the rigid routine and lifestyle, convincing ourselves it was a good method to learn self-discipline.

"John, how would you like to learn from both classes and work experience?" The administrator explained various job descriptions. "Would you be willing to accept the challenge of managing the bakery at first? Later, we'll transfer you to the vegetarian restaurant and the health-food store."

"If you'll guide me, I'll give it my best." In spite of my inexperience, I knew I had a keen mind, had potential, and cared about details. I felt elated at his confidence in me. I'd show him by being energetic and resourceful.

Turning to Sharon, he said, "I've got a job for you too. Would you be willing to work in the kitchen while you train to be a lifestyle counselor? The medical training will teach you to become a competent physician's assistant in the health center."

We were both thrilled with our work and amazed at the progress patients made on a good diet, plenty of exercise,

A Man of Authority

and hydrotherapy treatments. Sharon came home one day exclaiming, "God's simple remedies really work! I can't believe the miracles of healing we see with every new group of patients."

The physicians, a husband and wife, showed special interest in our progress, and I went out of my way to be cooperative and helpful. When I made mistakes, Dr. Martha treated me like a son, giving me counsel and making good suggestions. I admired her kind, gentle manner and could sense her confidence in and love for me.

Eventually, I noticed that the administrator was giving me more and more responsibilities. *Is he grooming me to be his assistant? Has he noticed I liked to meet and work with people?* I put forth extra effort to merit the added confidence he placed in me. After our first year, the institute invited me to be assistant administrator. I loved the challenge of leadership.

About a year later, an important board meeting convened. At its conclusion, Dr. Martha came to my office. "John, our administrator has accepted another position and will soon be leaving. We've noticed how well you have accepted and carried out the duties given you. You're familiar with the details of administration and have the dedication needed. Is this something you would consider?"

Then, speaking more like a mother than a physician, she added, "John, I have mixed feelings concerning your youth and lack of experience, but if you will stay in close communication with God and us, I'm sure we can work together harmoniously."

DARK LIGHT

So at twenty-three, I became the administrator, having several managers under me, many of them older and more experienced. I reveled in the authority that was now mine to participate in making important decisions. Until then, Sharon and I had worked in different departments, but we missed being together. Using my new authority, I now appointed her as my secretary and also as personnel manager. We loved being a team again.

"I need to make a diagram showing the chain of command for effective sharing of responsibility. Then each employee will understand to whom they answer. This will clarify that the final authority rests in the administrator," I told Sharon.

Just before I finished creating the diagram, the business manager left on a three-week vacation. While he was gone, I convinced the rest of the staff that these changes would be a more efficient way to run the institution.

"But one item disturbs me, Sharon," I admitted. "Up till now, the only one authorized to sign checks is the business manager/accountant. Certainly the administrator should also be authorized to sign checks."

"That's an item for the board to decide, isn't it? Then don't you have to take a copy of the action to the bank for authorization?"

"No problem. I'll get it cleared tonight at our executive committee meeting."

Later, I presented the business manager with my chain-of-command flowchart. He studied it for a long time. "Who authorized you to sign checks?" he finally asked. "It's never been done that way before."

A Man of Authority

"You're under a new administration now." I tried to sound pleasant as I added, "This change will make business matters flow more smoothly." The temperature in the room instantly chilled to subzero Arctic.

For a period of ten months, our patient count at the sanitarium was lower than usual. This shortage of income made it impossible for the institute to pay the workers their fifty-dollar-a-month stipend. The executive committee decided to give the workers extra vacation time as compensation. Because of our many financial needs, we decided to spend our vacation tree planting.

The first hour at work, Sharon ran into trouble. She constantly tripped on her long dress as she bent over. Several times she fell.

"John," Sharon complained as she lay sprawled on the ground, "I can't plant trees in this long dress. Surely God gave counsel in the Spirit of Prophecy about clothing that is still modest but more practical."

"Good idea. I'd enjoy a search of God's messages on dress reform. I'm sure there must be a balance that includes both modesty and convenience."

Every spare minute I had, I gathered convincing quotations on modesty, convenience, and healthful dress. All harmonized with biblical counsel. I compiled the material into an article titled "Pants for Women?"

"Read this, Sharon. Then let's go for a bicycle ride around the campus with you dressed as suggested."

She did, donning slacks with a shirt reaching to her hips. We created quite a stir as people saw us cycling. This gave me the opportunity I wanted. When asked, I shared

what I'd found. Some said, "Thanks, John. This additional light not only makes sense but is practical." Others, distressed and offended, condemned me. "John, you're compromising principles and letting down the standards! Can't you see that you're turning to the ways of the world?"

Even Dr. Martha confronted me. "John, our dress code is modest. We suggest well-fitting, good-quality, attractive attire. It is neither offensive nor out of style. You have a right to your own opinions—but not to circulate a paper stating that women may wear pants. It seems to me that even administrators should seek counsel with others before acting."

I wrote a letter on official institute stationery to the White Estate, with my research paper enclosed. Their response pleased me: "Your material is excellent. With your permission, we are placing it on our Question and Answer File, for we do get questions on women's dress frequently, and this will help in answering them."

Why, I wondered, *can't Adventist Christians come into unity and balance in Christ?* What I considered oppressive and domineering policies irked me. Though I knew I'd be castigated, I shared many copies with friends working at other self-supporting institutions.

I continued my personal campaign to change the policies of the institution. Many of the strict rules, such as the ban against pets, irritated me. In defiance, I bought a parakeet. My next campaign concerned what I considered the payment of an honest tithe. This time, I consulted the managers to see whether we could agree to change the institute's policy.

"As you know, our patient count has been down for some time. We haven't been able to pay stipends for ten months. I wonder if God is unable to bless us because we're not paying tithe on our housing, utilities, and food—which are included as part of our benefits.

"But if we do tithe the small stipend we receive, we'd have almost nothing left. How can we honor God by paying an honest tithe and still have money for our needs?" We all agreed to prove the Lord on this point by paying a faithful tithe on all our increase.

Almost immediately, our financial problems were reversed. The Lord blessed the institution financially so that soon we were able to increase the stipend from $50 a month to $80 a week. This victory reinforced my desire to bring about other reforms.

My next project concerned the lack of departmental accountability. Working closely with the managers, we put every department on a cost-effective budget program. When I counted all the changes I had implemented and compared our institution to similar institutions, I felt that ours was the most progressive and the most greatly blessed of God. Surely God favored me by trusting me with the most important work on the earth.

I also felt that God had blessed me with a superior understanding of the gospel. Whenever I read articles from various theologians who didn't express the truth as I understood it, I felt called of God to enlighten them.

One Sabbath afternoon as Sharon and I were reading the *Signs of the Times*, I exclaimed, "Listen to this." I read aloud a portion of an article. "I must write to the author and explain some essential truths he missed. If people continue to believe that they are covered by grace whenever they stumble and fall into sin, they'll never stop sinning, and Jesus will never be able to return."

After reading a few more pages, I added, "Here's another author who needs enlightenment. I can see where I can help him clarify and refine his theology too." Convinced that they would see the truth if it were presented to them, I began corresponding with well-known Adventist writers and evangelists.

But Sharon was less enthusiastic and began waving red flags with her questions. "John, are you sure that your position is right? Why do you have to be so picky on these fine points of justification?"

My response each time was to pull out my quotations. Using my best persuasive techniques, I gave her a "thus saith the Lord." She listened. Then, shaking her head, she would say, "Perhaps you're right."

About this time, a student arrived on campus who espoused what I considered a liberal theology. He believed that a person was still covered with Christ's righteousness while sinning. I immediately felt it my duty to set him straight. Eagerly, I began working on a quiz that I was sure would entrap him and enable him to see the flaws in his position. When the quiz was completed, I asked Sharon to type it for me. She read it through carefully. Instead of being delighted that I had done such a convincing job of making my position seem so right, she was deeply distressed by my quiz. "John," she exclaimed, "don't you

A Man of Authority

think you're taking this too far! This quiz isn't fair! I don't want to type it." Again, I pulled out my best persuasive techniques to convince her. Again, she reluctantly yielded.

At the beginning of our third year at the institute, we adopted our little daughter, Traci. Cuddling our new baby in one arm and hugging Sharon with the other, I exclaimed, "God is pouring His blessings on us. I love the challenges of my job–and now we have a precious baby."

As time went on, my responsibilities broadened. I served on the board of directors of four self-supporting institutions, so I traveled often. I also accepted preaching assignments in the surrounding churches.

I had deep convictions that our medical-missionary training school should be more closely tied to the Seventh-day Adventists Church. This position came to the forefront during my third and fourth years of administration.

Why must we persist in functioning independently from the Seventh-day Adventist denomination? Feeling competent to suggest a change, I called the department managers together to share my ideas. I felt proud of my proposal as I prepared my speech.

"We consider our institution a Seventh-day Adventist medical training school. Yet we do not have any accountability to the church. I've studied carefully the Madison-school system of organization that Mrs. White approved of in her day," I told them. "I do not find the authority for the system and plan of organization we have in our independent institutions today. We're not closely tied to the organized church. To whom are we accountable and re-

DARK LIGHT

sponsible? Only our own board. Joining together would increase the overall work of the church in maintaining order, discipline, unity, and cohesiveness."

I could see the men nodding their heads, agreeing with me. Encouraged, I continued.

"We could receive great benefit from the denomination's experience. We'd not only have the security of being part of the worldwide denominational workforce, but we'd also be protected by the organized church. Now we're just being tolerated by the church. Many Adventists look down on us as being second-rate institutions.

"It's my desire that we propose interdependence with local conference officers on our boards. I have already spoken with some who hold influential positions in the conference. They support the idea of our becoming an integral part of the denomination. Look at the pitfalls we'll avoid--extreme positions, faultfinding, and us-versus-them attitudes. True, we might have to move more slowly in making decisions. But it seems wiser for us to stay within the safety of the church instead of experiencing the freedom of independent action."

At about this time, Sharon, Traci, and I took a short vacation. Away from the institution, I had time to reflect on the possibilities of our institution adopting the changes I wanted to see in our working relationship with the church.

"Sharon, I no longer agree with the philosophy of self-supporting institutions. But I fear the opposition from Dr. Martha will be strong. I can't see the board consenting to make the changes needed to work with the conference without her approval. It's hopeless, useless! I feel I'm up against a brick wall. I've decided to write a letter of resignation."

When we returned, I gave my letter of resignation to Dr. George. I then heard through another source that the doctors had already removed me from my administrative position while I had been on vacation. Several of the managers who were sympathetic to our position encouraged me to withdraw my resignation and challenge the doctors' action.

About this time, both doctors left on business. Their absence gave us greater freedom to put our plans into action. We wrote a proposal that outlined an interdependent relationship with the conference that would require the doctors to step down from their positions. Most of the managers sided with my proposal. True, some workers objected. Sharp feelings surfaced. But in spite of opposition, I began the process of implementing these changes.

When the doctors returned, we presented them with our proposal.

"John, it is very painful for me to have to speak to you this way. I have loved you like a son." Dr. Martha had tears in her eyes. "Let me share with you why we removed you from your administrative position. I've sensed that you have harbored a spirit of rivalry against me and have acted unwisely. You've gone ahead on your own without taking proper counsel. Because of the division you have created on the staff, we feel we must ask you, and the managers working with you, either to cooperate or to sever all connections with us immediately."

Hurt and disappointed that my best efforts weren't appreciated, I shook my head. "I cannot continue to work here without accountability to the denomination."

Firmly, the doctors answered, "John, we're sorry. We cannot agree with your proposal."

And so we packed our belongings.

The Righteous Deceiver

Where could we go? We had saved only $300.

A friend knew of an Adventist minister in North Carolina who trained young men how to do evangelism using the Amazing Facts approach.

We contacted the minister, and he invited us to join the group. Putting aside my hurt feelings over being let go from the institute, I immersed myself in this new challenge.

"Use these Bible-study outlines, John," the pastor explained. "We'll alternate speaking appointments in the two churches that I pastor."

"Great," I said. I didn't mention my already-prepared sermons. With them I would convince the church members that if they were still sinning, they were lost. I was sure that God had given me the burden to make

the members of these two churches aware of their lost condition.

I did study the lessons the minister gave me. *My understanding of truth is beyond this*, I congratulated myself. *Using my unique approach to righteousness by faith, I can enlighten the Adventist Church. This is my chance to write a set of lessons using the research I've been doing these past years.*

Without telling the minister in charge, I developed nine lessons called "New Heart," based on Ezekiel 36:26, 27, which included an eleven-question quiz designed to spark interest and discussion. But my real motive was to determine whether the student understood my views on righteousness by faith or was deceived by what I felt were false, popular concepts.

After a few weeks, I announced to Sharon, "Several of the church members are excited over my views. When I go to their homes, they want to learn how to live a life of consistent victory over sinful thoughts, motives, and attitudes. Today, I presented my lesson on the gift of a new heart. While the head elder and I were studying, the pastor called on the phone. I wonder why he seemed surprised, almost suspicious, of why I was there."

When more requests came to study, I suggested that we meet on Sabbath afternoons—but I purposely neglected to inform the pastor. *Why should I feel guilty leading people to victory? Such an important message warrants these tactics.* Within a short time, I had a sizable following. It was exciting to work underground, like a secret agent, saving as many souls as possible before the pastor discovered I was teaching contrary to him. Like the Waldenses, I had to hide my "colors." No doubt God had chosen me to bring about both a revival and a reformation in these Adventist churches. I assumed the pastor would try to stop me from preaching the "truth," even though I had all the quotes and figured I could outargue him. So I worked with an urgency, fearing that my time was running out.

One Sabbath afternoon, the pastor drove past the church and saw all the cars in the parking lot. I saw his surprised expression as he walked into the room. He listened a while and then asked for a set of lessons.

I'd been working in North Carolina about five months when he called me to come to his office. He came right to the point. "John, I'm concerned about your extreme views on righteousness by faith. I'm even more concerned over a growing attitude in the members. It seems that the people in our churches are forming into two opposing camps. I fear that your teachings are creating conflict and debate. The unity we enjoyed before your arrival has disappeared."

He paused. I could feel my heart pounding in my throat and the blood rushing to my face. He pulled out the packet of my Bible lessons from a folder on his desk and continued, "I've carefully studied the lessons you wrote. I must admit that your approach is very subtle and clever, but there are parts that bother me. I'm especially concerned over the loaded questions you have put in your New Heart quiz. To ask Christians to make decisions like these seems to me to be very unfair. Both the quiz and lessons are not only divisive but also lead to unbalanced views of the great theme of righteousness by faith."

"But you know that Mrs. White says that most Adventists are living in a lost condition, still falling into sin," I countered. "When I realize that she says only one in twenty will be saved, I can only assume that most of our members are lost. So I'm emphasizing God's all-powerful hand to save them from sinning."

"But you are leaving out the important truth of His infinite pity and forgiveness," the pastor replied. "You're teaching only half of the truth. A growing Christian will be developing all the fruits of the Spirit. He'll be overcoming known sin by God's power. Yet the Bible teaches that within his heart there may be hidden or unconscious sins."

The pastor paused and looked very serious. "John, do not preach any more sermons on righteousness by faith. Please use your sharp, analytical mind and your persuasive talents to bring about unity and cooperation in the church. Will you work with us instead of against us?"

Stunned at his accusations, I answered, "Every lesson is based on Bible texts and sound doctrine leading the Christian to victory through the gift of a new heart. I believe my methods are right. God has something better for us than sinning and repenting. Can't you see that this will bring a revival in your churches?"

"No, John, I'm sorry to say that all I see now are confused members filled with suspicion, criticism, divisiveness, and un-Christlike debates. I've made an appointment to visit with the conference president next week. This will give you time to consider what I've said. Would you join me in prayer for God's guidance, wisdom, and blessings?"

After the prayer, I left to keep an appointment with a

The Righteous Deceiver

group of members waiting for another Bible discussion based on some of the quiz questions. I told them that the pastor had forbidden me to preach the "straight testimony"–that he wanted only doctrinal sermons. The news traveled fast. Soon a delegation went to the conference president to speak on my behalf.

In spite of my friends' pleadings that they had been greatly blessed by my ministry, the conference president's decision was firm. "John, I don't know whether you purposely planned to develop a party spirit. Nevertheless, in a very clever, cunning way, you presented an unbalanced picture of truth. These people say they have been blessed. However, in my opinion, this holier-than-thou attitude is a curse that has caused division and confusion, not harmony and unity. As I talked with the members, I didn't see the spirit of love manifest in preferring one another. Rather, they consider themselves 'righteous' and everyone else lost. Even the other intern with whom you worked has imbibed your spirit. Whether you have purposely planned it that way, only God knows. But we feel that you must leave this conference immediately. We're sorry that your methods and teachings have made this dismissal necessary."

Stunned, I went home and told Sharon, "We have no one to turn to but God. I cannot see where we've erred. Were we not teaching Bible truth? Have we not prayed to be led by His Spirit? Let's put God to the test," I suggested. "My sister Julie has invited us to visit her in southern California, but we have no money to travel. If God provides funds, we'll know He's guiding us and

that our teachings are from Him."

The next day, we received a letter in the mail from an unexpected source containing a check for $300.

Just before we left for southern California, we stopped to say goodbye to the pastor. I gave him this parting shot. "Obviously God is with us. We prayed for a sign. This money is an indication that we are following His will."

The older man laid his hand on my shoulder, "John, I don't think you understand what a loving Father you serve. Maybe God is saying, 'John, My boy, I love you even though I'm sad that you've been acting immaturely. You're still My child even if you're blinded to your faults—determined to go your own way, making serious mistakes. I respect your sincerity according to your understanding of right and wrong. I'll show My love by helping you when you call on Me.'"

But I chose not to listen to what the pastor said.

CHAPTER EIGHT

Me, Bring Unity?

Traci kept Sharon busy as I drove across the United States, pulling a four-by-six-foot trailer that contained all our possessions. Our little girl bounced and chattered, played games, and listened to stories. When she settled down for naps, Sharon and I tried to analyze the trend our lives had taken the past several years.

"John, I'm convinced there's something wrong with your 'rightness.' The endless hours you've spent studying the Bible and the Spirit of Prophecy shouldn't produce this kind of results. We've been dismissed from jobs twice in one year by people we respect and admire. And they wanted us to leave immediately! This makes me feel that our influence is poison to others. What's wrong with us?"

"I'm not sure," I admitted. "Once I believed error. You know–sinning and repenting–repeating the cycle end-

lessly. I even blamed God for not giving me victory over my sins. But this time, my emphasis is different. First, I help sinners see their lost condition. Then, I show them how, by faith, to accept a new heart. What follows is an experience of real victory over sin."

"John, you know I want to be a Christian, but I'm afraid to give my heart to God. I know that sooner or later I'll get impatient or upset again—and it's so discouraging to know that I've lost justification when that happens."

"But you can go to God immediately like I do and get saved again."

"I'm too weak, John. Besides, I think your salvation is based more on your strong works than on faith in Jesus. It's awful to live like this, without the peace and assurance of being saved."

"I believe God's promise in 1 Corinthians 10:13 that He'll make a way of escape," I continued. "But the promise is only for those who truly possess a new heart. Through faith in Jesus, I know Satan can never cause me to sin again without first gaining the consent of my will."

"So none of the power struggles you had as an administrator were sin? Could your pride of opinion be a demonstration of the sinful nature you condemn in others? John, truth has many sides. Maybe your ideas on righteousness by faith aren't complete. Something must be missing! Otherwise, you wouldn't cause division whenever you share them. There's a reason why people want to get rid of us!" Sharon started to cry.

"Honey, we've been over this dozens of times. I believe we're being persecuted for righteousness' sake. We need

Me, Bring Unity?

to 'rejoice and be glad,' as Jesus said."

"So I'm supposed to rejoice, knowing we messed up two good chances to work for God. Now we're heading for the West Coast with no idea of where we will live, with no job, and certainly with no positive job recommendations!"

"Just you wait. God has something special for us. I've asked Him to fulfill Jeremiah 33:3. I know He'll answer us and show us something wonderful that we don't know now."

When we arrived at my sister's home in California, her guest house had just been vacated. We'd just gotten settled in Julie's cabin in the hills above San Bernardino, when a friend called. "John, I've heard of a millionaire in Oregon who has a burden to sponsor people who'll do Bible work. I can give you his phone number. With your persuasive talents, maybe you can talk him into supporting you. I hear they're looking for a Bible worker at the church here in town."

I called the pastor. He confirmed the need for a Bible worker but added that the church had no budget to support one and that the conference didn't either.

"Let me pray about this, and I'll get back to you," I responded.

I called the wealthy businessman, who sounded most interested. "First, you must have the approval of your pastor. Have him contact me for details."

That Sabbath at church, I met the pastor and invited him to visit with us. We talked all afternoon.

"I'm going to be up front with you, John," he said. "Our church is split into two camps. Each wants someone from

DARK LIGHT

their theological camp to be head elder. We need a man of tact who is neutral. Someone who can bridge the gap, bringing the two sides into unity."

While he talked, my mind raced to the solution. I could bring them together. If both sides agreed with me and my New Heart theology, I could bring in unity. Not once did it occur to me that everywhere I'd been, my leadership had brought division.

Within a month, I had begun Bible studies with six non-Adventist families and had started a weekly meeting in the state prison, using the New Heart lessons.

One day, I received a phone call from the businessman. "John, as of this month, June 1984, you'll receive one thousand dollars a month from me. I'll support you for one year."

When I hung up, I turned to Sharon, "Need you wonder if God is with us? He kept His promise in Jeremiah 33:3. What a challenge we have for one year. I'm excited at the prospects." Within a few weeks, I was elected head elder and asked to serve on the social committee and school board. Sharon became a deaconess and the home-and-school leader. We both led out in the health emphasis for the Vacation Bible School. After serving on the nominating committee, I became acutely aware of the serious problems the disunity caused.

"Pastor," I said, "I'd like to take advantage of my position as head elder by striving to get total theological unity with the other elders on understanding the gospel. Then we can reach out to the deacons and deaconesses. That would be thirty-two people working in unity. We'll have

Me, Bring Unity?

weekend seminars called Lessons in Faith, using the New Heart lessons. What do you think about the idea?"

He smiled. "Anything to bring about unity. It's worth a try."

By October I had the support of the pastor and the leading members of the church. Then the pastor asked me to conduct the next twenty-one prayer meetings, using the Gospel of John. We baptized five, and I continued studying with three more, who asked to join the church. Responding to an ad in the newspaper, four additional persons requested studies.

In February the pastor suggested, "Would you share your message of faith with the deacon who has also led in the youth department? He's discouraged and hasn't come to church lately."

When I visited the deacon, he admitted, "I feel like a hypocrite with all my besetting sins."

"May we study the creative power of God's Word to uphold you when you're tempted? I'm sure your faith will increase, and you will be able to gain victory over your sins," I suggested. The deacon was soon back at church.

My friend Bob, who shared my views on theology, said, "John, I'm impressed to contact Gary Tyler, who was once our pastor here. He's not in the ministry now but is involved in an independent ministry in the Northwest. I want him to know these truths."

"Great! It makes me happy that God's last message will continue to bring hope and salvation to many."

By April I shared my fears with Sharon. "We have only one more month of financial support. How I hate to leave

DARK LIGHT

the twenty-two people I'm studying with each week, seven of whom aren't Adventists.

Sharon's answer surprised me. "Maybe God has other plans for us."

We didn't have long to wait. Emerald Health and Education Corporation, located in Loma Linda, needed a temporary missionary to replace a minister during his three-month furlough from Ireland.

If the General Conference approved, the corporation would send donated funds to the British Union to pay me for three months. Then, if my work was satisfactory, I might be given another position after the minister returned. The usual term of service was six years. "We've heard of your good work here," they continued. "Would you be willing to leave for Ireland about the first of July?"

"God's timing is perfect," I answered.

But I didn't qualify. I had only two years of college, and the denomination insisted that missionaries have at least a four-year degree.

Some time later, the leader telephoned again. "The need is so urgent that the corporation has decided to send you without an official General Conference call. Could you get ready to leave soon to pastor the small church in Galway, Ireland?" they asked.

"I'll talk with my wife and get back to you," I said.

Bursting into the house, I shouted, "Sharon, are you ready to be a missionary in the Emerald Isle?"

Sharon smiled. "You know I'll go anywhere with you. But I have one concern." She paused and gave me a pleading look. "Sure, I'll go to Ireland, John, but I'd like to stay

Me, Bring Unity?

there too. Maybe this time we could finish the task God has called us to do. I don't want to be asked to leave. John dear, let's pray that we can live out Philippians 2:3. Would you read it?"

I thought I heard God speaking as I read, "Do nothing out of selfish ambition or vain conceit, but in humility consider others better than yourselves" (NIV).

"Just think of how wonderful our life would be, living in unity with others, preferring them above ourselves instead of our independent judgment." She came close and hugged me, whispering, "And, sweetheart, that depends on you."

Can't Pin Me Down

We arrived on the misty green island with no money, no car, and no place to live. "Sorry, honey," I said. "We'll have to make do in one little room in the schoolhouse for a while. And we're in for plenty of rain."

"I know. A brochure I picked up at the airport says that the average rainfall here is between sixty to one hundred inches a year," Sharon groaned. "That means I've got to keep Traci in this tiny room."

"I'm glad I brought my rain gear. I'll strap my Elmo machine, my Bible studies, and my Bible on the ten-speed bike that's out in the shed. That's the way I'll meet the people."

Each night, I came home through rain to torrents of tears. Gloomy, wet weather and cramped, inconvenient living conditions make a little girl with no place to play

DARK LIGHT

cranky. That, along with no friends nearby, sparked waves of homesickness for Sharon.

"Give me time, dear. Maybe after I get involved and make friends, it will be easier," she said through her tears.

The first Sabbath, I drove around the town, picking up members in the church's big van. There were only eighteen of us. As one woman settled in the back seat with her children, she gasped, "Am I glad Jesus' righteousness covers me! I acted like the devil trying to get the kids ready for church."

Immediately, I thought, *She needs to understand the gospel. That's not Christianity. Jesus doesn't cover our sins when we fail like that.*

Right away, I began my sermons on righteousness by faith. Several families eagerly studied the New Heart lessons with me.

Because most Irish people are strong Catholics, I needed a new approach for the general public. An article in the local paper gave me an idea. It read, "Ireland, with Scotland and England, has the highest incidence of heart disease in the world. Such disease is responsible for four out of every ten deaths in this country. The irony is that we can change it by altering our eating habits and lifestyle."

Immediately, Sharon and I began to develop a wellness program. Using advertisements and fliers, I announced: "Upon your request, an experienced Lifestyle Counselor will present this program in the privacy of your home. Natural remedies, vegetarianism, stress management, and a stop-smoking plan will be included in this course."

In a short time, we had more home calls than we could handle. When the minister returned, we moved to the Shannon church near Limerick. He and I worked closely together. As I shared my views on righteousness by faith with the pastor, he showed sincere interest, though his wife did not. After five months, the mission showed its confidence in us by beginning to pay us as regular workers.

Our work in Shannon had a positive start. From an ad we put in the newspaper, fifty people showed up for our thirteen-week Wellness Seminar. Each week, we discussed a new health habit for them to practice, and, of course, we slipped in thoughts from the Bible.

As a result of these health seminars, I soon had twenty-two non-Adventists studying the Bible in their homes with me each week. We used a revised version of the New Heart lessons that I called New Heart Stress-Management Course.

At the end of session number five, a well-to-do couple in their late thirties came to me, stating, "We're certainly not gong to become Bible-thumping vegetarians!" But they kept attending. By the end of the series, this now-vegetarian couple wanted me to come to their home and give them Bible studies.

Another man stated, "I'm not interested in your Bible studies. You're just wasting your time."

I changed the subject and asked, "Do you have any health problems?"

"Do I? No one can help my severe stomach pain.

DARK LIGHT

Wouldn't be talking to you now if I hadn't just taken pain medicine. I'm on disability. Can't even go out and play with my kids."

"I think I can help you. May I try?"

"How much do you charge?"

"Since I'm not a medical doctor and use only natural remedies, the price is free."

"Well, I've got nothing to lose. Let's give it a try."

I did a lifestyle analysis and found that he was violating almost every natural law of health. As I taught him and his family the eight laws of health, they began improving their diet and, over time, followed each natural law.

After discussing diet, I offered to give the man hydrotherapy treatments.

"I'll try it if you think it'll do any good," he assented.

"I'll need the entire family to help," I requested. I gave the fomentations. Their son held the clock and timed the alternating application of heat and ice. The daughter kept his footbath hot, and the little one put cold cloths on his forehead.

We had a great time working together. After three treatments, his wife knew how to proceed without my instruction. Soon they did a better job than I did.

Following each treatment, I suggested we put charcoal politices on his stomach. Each time, he objected, "But we can't buy charcoal powder here, only charcoal sticks."

At my request, they finally purchased some charcoal sticks. The entire family watched as I put the charcoal in a bag, ran over it with the van, and then pounded the charcoal with a sledgehammer. Finally, I poured the charcoal into a blender to pulverize it into powder. After four or five weeks of treatment and improved lifestyle, the man was off all drugs and could move around without pain. By then, the family was open to Bible studies. In time, the entire family was baptized.

A veterinarian came to me saying, "I can't sleep. I've been on sleeping pills for years, yet I never feel rested."

I assured him that if he followed what the lifestyle seminar taught, he would sleep better.

"Anything to get away from this," he responded. Soon he was sleeping like a baby. "What else does the Adventist Church have to offer?" he asked.

After one happy, successful year, we returned to the United States for a four-week vacation. My friend Bob, from southern California, invited us to meet him at Soquel Camp Meeting in central California. He wanted to tell us of their incredible success in bringing people to experience victory over sin.

After we'd chatted for a while, Bob said, "Let me show you how our program works." We began to walk across the campground but had not walked far when he stopped a stranger and asked, "Would you like God to give you complete victory over your sins? He's done this for me. I've found joy and peace I've never known before."

"Sure, I'd like to be done with sin," the man replied.

"You may have it now if you will just accept Jesus into your heart." Bob explained the meaning of righteousness by faith. When he finished, he and the stranger knelt right there in the open. The man believed, gave his heart to God, and went away praising God. I was impressed when

this sequence happened again and again.

Upon returning to Ireland, I felt compelled to sharpen the tone regarding this wonderful truth in my sermons and personal work. Soon the president of the mission, Elder Southcott, heard of my sermons on righteousness by faith and perfection. In January 1986, I received a letter from him.

> Dear John,
> The mission committee met yesterday to discuss some of the unrest that certain of your theological views have aroused in the hearts and minds of your members. . . . I believe you to be sincere. I know that you would not wish your views to have an unfortunate effect upon either the organization or members and workers.
> I would like you to give me a condensed version of your views as they relate to the fundamental beliefs of the church. In the meantime, we are asking the pastor in Galway to be responsible for the Shannon church also. Please concentrate on your health-outreach programs rather than on membership nurture. We will arrange to meet you soon and hear your views on these issues.
> W. Southcott, President

Sharon burst into tears when she read the letter. "Oh, John, I've begged you to soften your appeals. I've urged you not to be so harsh and specific on the fine points of righteousness by faith. Why must you always make so prominent your views on controversial subjects like perfection? You could be more tactful and less dogmatic."

"Doesn't Ezekiel say to cry aloud and spare not?" I countered.

"But what good will your message do in Ireland if we get kicked out here too? Everything's been going so well, and now this. Maybe you need to learn to cooperate with your employers and your church. They have insights that you don't. How many times you've tried to outargue me. The only reason I give in to you is that you're the leader, and I assume you're having a closer walk with God than I am. So I yield to your opinions, thinking they must be more in accord with the truth than mine. Now, what are you going to do?"

"Seems like I'd better write a letter to answer the president's questions on my views." I took out a sheet of paper and began a first draft. "How does this sound for an introduction, Sharon?

" 'As a young and inexperienced gospel worker, I am acutely aware of my inadequacies and the errors in judgment that I make. I pray that God will make up for my deficiencies and grant me humility and a teachable spirit so that I can turn my mistakes into victory.' "

"Sounds pretty humble, John, but do you mean it? Are you really willing to submit to their judgment?"

"About as much as Martin Luther was willing to recant when the church accused him of heresy!"

"Just what I thought. In other words, you have no intention of cooperating."

"Not when I know I'm right. How can they convince

me otherwise, when I have so many quotations to back me up? But I'll drive to Belfast on the date they suggested and act as submissive as I can without compromising truth."

By the time I finished my letter to the conference president, I felt confused. "Sharon, I need to take a walk and to think. I'm going to hike to the domes."

For three miles, I walked up the emerald green hills above the town of Limerick to the huge radar domes. As I enjoyed the beautiful Irish countryside, I talked with God.

"Sometimes I feel unnerved, God, for I don't know where to go or what to do if I'm asked to leave Ireland. Yet I'm convinced I'm one of the few to whom You have revealed this wonderful truth of complete victory. Didn't You call me to share this message with all who will listen and understand?"

I didn't hear God's affirmation, but I felt confident of His leading. I looked forward to the challenge of being asked to discuss my messages with the president at Belfast. Because I knew I had truth on my side, I was sure no one could dissuade me from it.

Finally, the day came. After a cordial visit, the president sent me home with a list of questions that he wanted me to answer. I answered truthfully, yet evasively. I was going to make it hard for the conference to oust me. Elder Southcott later commented to Paul, the minister from Galway, "I can't seem to pin him down."

Separation

Not long after my trip to Belfast, my friend and fellow minister from Galway dropped by. I felt close to him, and our working relationship had been great!

"John, let's talk a bit," Paul said.

"Sure. What's on your mind?"

While he hesitated, I could feel his concern. "John, God has greatly blessed our joint ministry here in Ireland. I've been stimulated by your fresh, new ideas and analytical mind. You've given me some real treasures from your study of the Spirit of Prophecy. You're steady, not impulsive. I admire your self-control, self-discipline, and self-confidence. How you stay unruffled and don't get upset by what others say amazes me. This gives you lots of credibility."

I interrupted him. "Something's bothering you, Paul, what is it"

DARK LIGHT

"OK. But first I want you to know that you're a pleasant mixture of being easy to work with and being a challenge. I like being on your team. I'm thrilled over the tremendous success you and Sharon have had in the wellness seminars."

He pulled a letter from his coat pocket. "You got a copy of this letter from Belfast too. That's why I'm upset. The president says you've been relieved of your pastoral duties, and he's asked me to take all Sabbath sermons. Seems you've created unrest and disquiet among the members because of your extreme views and independent spirit."

I tried not to show my hurt but answered in a calm, quiet voice, "Maybe the president's charge should be considered more positive than negative, Paul. Suppose a man believed that Sabbath keeping wasn't important. Then someone came along and taught the Ten Commandments. Wouldn't he experience unrest until he surrendered? Unrest could be a sign that the minister is doing his job and that the Holy Spirit is bringing conviction to hearts."

"Come on, John. Don't pass this over with your smooth logic. Perfection as the Bible teaches brings joy and comfort. But your views are discomforting. They foster disunity. I know; I've been visiting the members too. They're confused, bewildered. I don't attack your views, but try to complement them and bring balance. I point them to victory through Jesus, too, but with a different emphasis. Your ideas negate Christ's merciful forgiveness. You stress that if a person sins, he or she hasn't been converted and isn't a Christian. I agree that we cannot limit what Christ

Separation

can do in us and through us. But His call for righteousness is always blended with mercy. What you teach is only partial truth–and that makes it dangerous and in error!"

"I disagree. Don't the inspired messages say that only one in twenty of our church members are prepared to meet God? That means most of them are lost. Shouldn't I warn them and present hope for victory? They appreciate it too. I told them about the president's letter. Then I prepared a three-page anonymous evaluation, asking for their opinions. They've said what they believe–their perception of my ministry. Here, listen to this one."

I proceeded to read one of the responses. " 'We've learned and understood righteousness by faith from John's sermons in a way that can only have been inspired by the Lord. For this we shall be eternally grateful. This is our most significant spiritual awakening since learning the Adventist message years ago.' "

Paul sighed with disappointment. "How could you, John? Revealing that which you know will work against the conference, your employer. That's not only disloyal and unethical, but it causes disunity. And asking for a personal evaluation of yourself doesn't seem to harmonize with Paul's counsel, 'Do nothing out of selfish ambition or vain conceit, but in humility consider others better than yourselves' [Philippians 2:3, NIV]."

I almost felt like the kid caught with his hand in the cookie jar. Paul had never confronted me like this before. I tried the defensive method. "You know I'm never vindictive, nor do I take offense when you disagree with me."

"That's part of the problem, John. Because we're fac-

ing a crisis and I care so much, I'm going to be open and blunt. Armed with quotes and a gracious but holier-than-thou attitude, you never budge! You refuse to argue, because you're so sure you're right, so sure you are the final authority! Your perfectionist views show up in your lifestyle. Sometimes you hardly seem human. No one works harder than you do, but you seem so cold, so impersonal, above bitterness, almost above all emotion. I can't say you're unloving, but there's no warmth. You're not pushy. Just confident, persuasive, and persistent in your stubborn, quiet way. Because you're so articulate, so logical, and so sincere, you exert a strong influence on people. But, John, could you be leading them into deception?"

I felt dizzy, reeling under his blows. *Is he right?* I wondered. *Do I really have a Messiah complex? How can my good friend misunderstand me? Obviously God has given me victory over pride, resentment, unholy ambition, vanity, and anger. Maybe I'm again being persecuted for righteousness' sake.*

Paul continued to unload on me.

"You've shared with me your voluminous correspondence with dedicated ministers like George Vandeman, Joe Crews, H. M. S. Richards Jr., and others. I'm concerned, John, with your supreme confidence. Do you honestly believe that everyone else is either wrong or inconsistent, and only you have the whole truth?" We sat in silence for several minutes, Paul's chin in his hands.

Looking up, he pleaded, "John, we all love you–your church members, the conference officers, me. We know how God has blessed your work with the public in health

Separation

evangelism. I'd be happy to go to the committee on your behalf if you'll just cooperate. But unless you soften your dogmatic messages and extreme views, I fear you'll be on your way to the States in two weeks."

"Paul, my trust in God is firm and sincere. How could He bless so much if I were not following His leading?" I asked. "Could it be that Satan sees the great burden I have to expand the medical-missionary work in Ireland? Because he knows it will open doors for the gospel, maybe he's using leaders in the Adventist Church to prevent this."

"John, think of the blindness of Christ's disciples. If they'd had their way, they'd have made Jesus king. But over and over again, Jesus restrained them. His actions and words went unheeded. Their pride and ambition were all wrapped up in their wrong ideas of truth. But Jesus didn't abandon them in their error. He knew they must fall to the depths before they could understand. John, I fear you're blind too. Like the disciples, you won't allow words to change you, but God may permit you to fall very low."

Paul walked to the door and opened it. "I hope I can do something to prolong your stay in Ireland," he said as he shut the door behind him.

We were allowed to stay until July 1987, completing two years of the six in our original assignment. Because of a generous moving allowance from the conference and the sale of our car and used furniture, along with the favorable dollar-pound exchange, we left Ireland with $17,000 cash. The Emerald Foundation also offered to pay the expenses for me to finish my college degree. I refused their generous offer because a passage I had read in *Testimonies for the Church* led me to believe that the only training I needed was the unction of the Holy Spirit.

During the last month, I helped with the transition of Bible studies and health classes to my replacement, a doctor and his wife. They didn't agree with my views on salvation. So in my farewell sermon at Shannon, I warned the church members, "Be on guard for wolves in sheep's clothing. If anyone teaches a gospel other than I have preached, beware. Why, even if I should return with another gospel, don't accept it. You will know it is error."

Were my words prophetic?

Back in the States, I applied for work as a Bible instructor in several conferences, but there were no openings. We paid cash for a $20,000 motor home and decided to visit friends, sharing our message of victory through faith. Our first stop was at the southern California church where we had worked. Excited over additional light on the faith of Jesus, our friends urged us to help them start a new ministry.

"John, you're all set up to travel. God brought you back to spread the message all over the United States. You can bring hope to Adventists who are still sinning. What a challenge! You'll lead them to experience instant victory over all sin and also assure them they'll never lose this experience. Never sin again! Just trust in the power of God!"

"Look, guys! Aren't you going a bit too far?" I asked.

Separation

"Are you saying you're sinless?"

"Isn't God's hand all powerful? Didn't Jesus come to save us from all sin? Go study this out for yourself."

I accepted their challenge to do additional research. The quotation that impressed me most came from an Ellen G. White *Signs* article. "Your only safety is in coming to Christ, and ceasing from sin this very moment. The sweet voice of mercy is sounding in your ears today but who can tell if it will sound tomorrow" (*Signs of the Times*, 29 August 1892).

Using my research, I wrote a powerful paper on the faith of Jesus. The thesis of the article was that if we truly take hold of the same faith Jesus exercised, we'll have the same victory He had. All depends on *our ability* to truly take hold of His faith.

Four of us men–Bob, Rick, Kevin, and I–joined with Gary Tyler, who'd been a minister in southern California but who now worked in the northwest. Gary's mission was to reach Adventists with the message that they could have victory over sins that had plagued them for years. He based his theory on the passage that states, "Whosoever is born of God doth not commit sin" (1 John 3:9).

Our message brought about division wherever it was presented. At first, we had no intention of separating from the Seventh-day Adventist Church. Soon, however, we developed an us-versus-them attitude. From there, it took only a small step to separate from the Seventh-day Adventist Church.

One of our leaders applied Jesus' warning to beware

of the leaven of the Pharisees to the Seventh-day Adventist Church. "Only if we meet separately can we be free from the denomination's leavening influence," Gary warned. "I fear the hypocrisy of those not living what they believe. We must not be contaminated by their errors, which could leaven our faith.

"I'm convinced that apostasy and worldliness have turned the Adventist Church into the harlot of Revelation. The apostasy is evident by intemperance, divorces, jewelry, and many other sins. If the SDA ministers preached from the 'pure fountain,' they'd deal with these sins. We're forced to admit that the church has become Babylon." Gary's firmness startled me. "We must heed the call, 'Come out and be separate.' The gates of hell have prevailed against the organized church. God's counsel forces us to separate from all confused and unbelieving persons."

"Let's not move so fast," I objected. "As a seventh-generation Adventist, I'm not about to leave what I firmly believe to be God's church. Only if a javelin were thrown at me, like Saul threw at David, would I leave the 'palace.' "

The next day, Bob cornered me with a new argument. "What's to be feared more, physical javelins or spiritual javelins? John, aren't our converts already dodging javelins of unbelief from members who've rejected our message?"

I agonized. *Is he right, or am I falling into a crevice of self-deception?* A few days later, I found my answer in the Ellen G. White *1888 Materials* collection. "A reformation must go through the churches.... As reformers they had come

Separation

out of the denominational churches, but they now act a part similar to that which the churches acted. We hoped that there would not be the necessity for another coming out" (356, 357).

How providential, I decided, *that God would encourage us at the beginning of another coming out, letting us know we're on track.*

Another statement totally convinced even me that our group must separate from the Seventh-day Adventist Church. Concerning the apostle Paul, Ellen G. White stated, "Fearing that the faith of the believers would be endangered by continued association with these opposers of the truth, Paul separated from them and gathered the disciples into a distinct body" (*The Acts of the Apostles*, 286).

The weekend we made the final decision to separate, I had a specific answer to prayer. I felt impressed to ask God to heal my TMJ (temporomandibular joint) joint disorder. For years, my jaw would click when I chewed. Often it locked closed, preventing me from getting even a fork into my mouth. My jaw would open only after I gave it a good knock. In answer to my prayer, God healed my TMJ disorder. Since that day, it has never bothered me. "Surely this miracle is evidence we have God's approval," I told Sharon.

"But, John, could we be deceived in thinking God's goodness and blessings are proof we're right theologically?" she asked. "Wouldn't a merciful God answer the prayers of His children even when they believe error?" I had no answer for her.

That same weekend, we had a strategy meeting to plan

how to spread the urgent message to call out God's children from the fallen Seventh-day Adventist Church.

Gary turned to me. "John, you have a way of convincing people. You and Sharon need to travel all over the United States." Then to Kevin, Bob, and Rick, he added, "You will need to travel too. What a privilege to proclaim this last message to call out God's people for translation. I'll stay here at headquarters."

We began our coast-to-coast itinerary with a weekend at a self-supporting school in Washington. My Friday-evening message challenged, "You have only one option—victorious Christian living, a free gift that may be yours immediately if you desire it."

On Sabbath, I delicately presented the second angel's message, the need for separation from Babylon. Several sincere people who had been disappointed in the lack of true godliness in the church joined us. In our message they saw something better–truths they wanted. Among the group, I rebaptized two teacher families on Sunday morning. This caused real trouble with the rest of the faculty and almost closed down the school. Still, I felt rewarded that we could save at least two families.

We had similar success baptizing staff members at an academy in Oklahoma. By focusing on our task–preparing a people for translation–we overlooked the agony we caused when families split.

Our message attracted many, such as the large group in Wenatchee, Washington. "We want to be baptized in the Columbia River today," they insisted.

Thinking of their comfort, I pointed out, "But it's bit-

Separation

terly cold, with a strong wind blowing."

Seeing their disappointment, Sharon suggested, "John, go forward in faith. I'll pray that God will take away the clouds, calm the wind, and cause the sun to shine."

"Then let's drive to the river now." I started for our motor home as I buttoned my overcoat. At the river's edge, the large group of candidates huddled together for protection from the wind. Sharon stood to one side, praying silently. As I led the first candidate into the water, the wind suddenly stopped, and the sun shone bright and warm. Its bright rays seemed to confirm God's blessings on our ministry. Not until the last person and I walked out of the water did the clouds again cover the sun and the cold wind begin to blow.

When all those baptized had changed into dry clothes, we stood by the river singing hymns. I saw tears of joy streaming down many faces. "This must be a glimpse of what it will be like to sing together beside the river of life," exclaimed a newly baptized man.

"What precious fellowship we enjoy!" I agreed. "We're enjoying a little bit of heaven on earth."

Was the latter rain being poured out? Was the power we experienced going to take the world? Each month, we baptized scores of people–in oceans, lakes, rivers, swimming pools, even bathtubs. Because I was in the water so often, I purchased fisherman's waders to keep out the cold.

For almost two years, we enjoyed a tremendous spiritual high, thriving on bringing so many to this new experience of total victory.

DARK LIGHT

"John, have you noticed that my Christian life is no longer a cycle of ups and downs?" Sharon asked one day.

"Indeed I have. Your discouragement is gone, and you radiate joy."

"And I can even see blessings in every trial," Sharon rejoiced. "John, I'm growing in Christ. I'm seeing new heights to attain. There's no stopping point."

Our message attracted a variety of people. It appealed to those who liked sensational ideas and exciting teachings. Tired of the isolation they had experienced in the church, loners came. Considered nobodies before, they gladly accepted positions of responsibility in our church. Some new Adventists gladly joined our church, thriving on the fellowship. However, most who joined with us were deep students of the Spirit of Prophecy. Many of them had been leaders in their local churches.

We headed our motor home to the medical missionary training center in the South where I'd been fired as administrator. Knowing that we wouldn't be welcomed on the campus, we decided to visit the people we knew in the community.

We chose to visit a blind man and his wife first. They eagerly accepted our teaching and added a challenge of their own. "Wouldn't it be wonderful if God would give me sight when I'm rebaptized!" the man suggested. "He could heal me now just as easily as Jesus healed the blind so long ago."

"According to your faith, be it unto you," I answered.

"I do believe! Didn't Jesus say, 'Ask and it shall be done unto you'? Just think of the glory to His name and

Separation

the message we bear when word goes out that I can see again!" he exclaimed.

I decided to return to my motor home to pray and think about his suggestion. My mind raced as I told Sharon, "Just think how this would convince the skeptics. If God heals this man, all the people at the institute–including the doctors–would know that our message comes from God. Maybe then they'd quit opposing us and be willing to listen. Our movement would be vindicated. What a terrific breakthrough!"

I hurried back to the home of the blind man. "Yes, let's put God to the test by telling everyone of your request. God willing, you'll be a modern Bartimaeus. Let's record the service on videotape to verify the miracle."

My heart pounded wildly as I immersed the man, expecting to hear his shout, "Praise God. I can see!"

When he came up out of the water, he looked up in silence. "I think I saw a flash of light," he groaned. "But now all is as dark as before."

Why didn't God give him sight? Was our faith too weak? Was the man still a sinner, and only God knew? Or was God trying to reveal my true motives? Not once did I suspect pride. After all, wasn't I God's messenger, sent to prove the rightness of our movement?

The Victory-Now Message

"We're planning to have a camp meeting at Lassen Volcanic National Park in California in July," Gary announced. "This is a beautiful spot. We're expecting a large crowd from all over the United States and Canada. Many will join our church in baptism. Plan to attend." We were having a planning session at our northern Idaho headquarters.

Then he called me aside. "John, we've scheduled you to preach the first and the last sermons at the camp meeting." Pleased, I looked forward to this spiritual feast.

A few weeks later, we headed south to Hat Creek Campground in Lassen Park. Traveling with us in our motor home was Traci's beautiful, long-haired Persian Chinchilla cat, which we'd brought back from Ireland. She never went outside and probably had no idea she was a cat. Once when a mouse slipped out from under the sink,

she merely reached out and tapped it with her paw.

Somehow our beloved pet escaped. For four days, we searched everywhere and joined Traci in praying for the cat's safe return. Though we'd nailed posters on many trees in the campground, no one had seen her. Early in the morning on the day before we had to leave, a man pounded on our door. "On my morning walk, I just saw a white cat sitting in the sun," he said. "I rushed to your camper. Follow me."

We dashed out, but when we got to the rock, no cat was in sight. I called and called. No response. Returning to the rock, I sat down to pray. At that moment, I spotted two or three long white hairs with black tips. Sure that our cat had scraped the sharp rock edges, I crawled around the rock. There I saw an opening like a tiny cave. Two green eyes stared out of the blackness at me. I reached into the cave and grabbed the cat. God had answered our prayers.

Carrying the cat back to the motor home, I came to the conclusion that this experience must be an acted parable containing instructions from God. I now had the subject for my final sermon, "The Lost Shall Be Found." For some time, we'd been convicted that the honest believers in Europe must be warned. Now God had given us the answer. We would be the first overseas missionaries of our movement, urging the lost on that continent to accept our message of "victory now" through faith in Jesus.

That Sabbath afternoon, Kevin and I thrilled with joy as we baptized more than two hundred people. That same afternoon, a generous offering provided funds for a missionary trip to Europe.

A short time later, we shipped two motor homes to

The Victory-Now Message

England. Bob, Irene, Karen, Sharon, Traci, and I joined forces for this final assault for God.

For two weeks, we labored for souls in England. Many whom we contacted from the "fallen religion of Adventism" refused to accept our message of the "faith of Jesus." At the end of the two weeks, we reluctantly paused outside the Country Life Restaurant, where our pleas for its employees to leave the church had been refused.

"Let us do as Jesus commanded," I said. "Whosoever will not receive you . . . shake off the very dust from your feet as a testimony against them."

I felt relieved after the foot-shaking episode. "Obviously God has no more true children in England. None desire to be called out of Babylon. Let's take a ferry across the North Sea to Belgium."

"But, John, we have no contacts there as we did in England. How can we find those who are faithful and true?" Sharon objected.

"No problem," Bob, our co-leader, reassured. "You know how people stop and stare at our large motor homes. They can't help but notice us as we drive through Belgium. We'll stop now and then in prominent places such as Brussels to make ourselves available. The Holy Spirit will speak to honest hearts and send them to us. When they ask why we're in their country, we know they'll be open to receive our message. God knows who His children are. Can't we trust Him to finish His work?"

Sharon looked dubious. "Are you sure that's the method Jesus used? Didn't He go to the people to seek and save the lost?"

DARK LIGHT

"We have a perfect Bible example to follow," I, the theologian of the group, interrupted.

"What do you mean?" I could see that Sharon felt uncomfortable with Bob's idea.

"Remember how God saw the faithful eunuch as he read from the scroll of Isaiah? Didn't God hear the cry of his heart for help and miraculously send Philip to him? Can't He do the same for us?" I replied confidently.

"If I remember the story correctly, Philip ran to him, not the eunuch to Philip." Sharon paused to make her point. Neither of us answered. Backing down, she muttered, "If you men think this is the best method to give the final warning to all of Belgium, I'll submit."

"Look at the people staring at our motor homes," Traci said as we drove slowly through Belgium. But no one came to talk to us–even when we stopped to pray.

"Lord," we pleaded, "send the power of the Holy Spirit to impress Your honest-hearted children to come to us. Create in them a desire to hear the final message."

For two days, we drove through the major cities and towns. We parked a long time at a rest stop on the freeway just outside of Brussels. Still no one came. Was the Holy Spirit's call falling on deaf ears?

Later that day, we again pulled to the side of the road. Standing beside our motor homes, Bob asked, "We're almost ready to cross into Germany. Shall we move on?"

"God knows we've spent two days pleading for opportunities to give the warning call of the three angels' messages to Belgium," I answered. "Because no one has stopped us, I conclude God has no children in this country who'll obey

The Victory-Now Message

the urgings of the Spirit. Surely He's finishing the work quickly, as He promised. 'For He will finish the work and cut it short in righteousness, because the Lord will make a short work upon the earth' " [Romans 9:28, NKJV].

Bowing my head, I prayed with great pathos, "God, we commit Belgium to the final judgment. We understand Your heartbreak as You left the lost city of Jerusalem."

But even as I said "Amen," a strange doubt entered my mind. *Are we really doing as Jesus did?* I pushed the doubt aside.

Irene, one of our group, spoke German. "I have contacts with prominent leaders, even a former president of the Reformed Adventist Movement. Surely this group will accept our message. I'm sure we can rebaptize them into God's chosen remnant church."

With renewed zeal, we entered Germany. We had not driven far when we came to a beautiful, scenic town. "Let's stop and ask God to show us what to do and where to go," Sharon suggested.

Almost as soon as she finished praying, a man drove up and stopped. In broken English, he asked, "Do you want to know where to park? I can help you."

He seemed like an angel sent from God as he led us to a secluded spot. Here we had both water and septic services available. From this base, we branched out into other areas of Germany and even into France.

It was here on that morning in 1989 that we shared those dreadful dreams–Irene's dream of total darkness in the tunnel and my dream of gulping rotten orange juice. Terrible forebodings filled our minds as each waited for the other to speak. Finally, Sharon asked, "Do you think the Lord could

be sending us a message to turn back from what we are doing? Could what we think is truth have some poison in it?"

"But, Sharon," I objected with vigor, "you know how often we've asked for guidance. If we're not guided by God, why would He answer so many of our prayers? He's even performed miracles on our behalf. Many have received great joy and happiness in accepting instant victory through Christ. If we weren't doing His will, wouldn't He have stopped us? And we're not finished, for our primary reason for coming to Europe is to go back to Ireland, where we worked for two years. We have many friends in those Adventist churches whom I know will accept our message and be ready to meet Jesus. No, we must press on!"

I spoke with conviction. Sharon, usually ready to submit, tried again. "John, could there be another viewpoint? Remember the letter we received from our friends in Ireland just before we left the States? They asked us not to come."

Though the letter was disappointing, I had an explanation. "And you know why? My sister Janet wrote that we were no longer loyal Seventh-day Adventists but had joined a deceptive offshoot. I can't understand why Janet has forsaken this precious message and left our movement."

Sharon watched me slump on the sofa as she washed the dishes. I hoped that my face didn't reveal my inward confusion. But it was a struggle to maintain my usual enthusiasm. "No, Sharon. We must go forward! I'm not ready to turn back! I wrote to our friends that I'd pray each day that when we arrive in Ireland, they will come and greet us with the words, 'Blessed are they that come in the name of the Lord.'"

But would they?

We Belong Nowhere

My heart pounded with a mixture of fear and joy at the familiar sights of Shannon, the city I loved. *Why do doubts keep surfacing? Am I really on God's mission?* Memories of people dear to our hearts from the two years we'd pastored there surfaced as we drove toward our former home. Our closest friends had moved into the house where we'd lived. As we parked our motor homes in the familiar driveway, I saw the door open. Would they accept us?

"John, Sharon, welcome!" They ran to us with open arms.

That evening, Connie confided, "I'm concerned. I fear I've lost my first love. My life has too much sin, too few victories."

"And that's why we came–to offer you continual victory. Since we left, we've grasped by faith that oneness with the

DARK LIGHT

Father for which Jesus prayed in John 17. He has seated us in heavenly places with Christ. As it did for Jesus, sin has lost its appeal. How wonderful to have our humanity and His divinity blended so closely that wherever we are, it is as if the Father is speaking through us."

Connie looked dubious. "You're our former pastor, and we trust you, John, but haven't you gone too far? You know the danger–when we choose to be independent and separate from the brethren in the church, we risk self-deception. Even the most sincere can listen to the wrong voice. Isn't it a bit extreme to suggest that you are almost like God?"

"Listen, Connie, I can prove every word of our message of complete victory from the Bible and the Spirit of Prophecy," I assured her. "Your only safety is in coming to Christ and ceasing from sin this very moment. The sweet voice of mercy is sounding in your ears today, but who can tell if it will sound tomorrow."

For the next two hours, I poured out an avalanche of convincing statements. Heedless of the turmoil and heartache I might bring to the Shannon church, I zealously pressed both Connie and her sister, one of the church-school teachers, into believing our movement was God's true church. I repeatedly showed them evidence that the Adventist Church had become fallen Babylon.

"But, John, I love my church. I can't bear to leave those so dear to my heart."

The time had come to persuade Connie with my most successful tool. This method had influenced hundreds to leave the Seventh-day Adventist Church and join our movement.

We Belong Nowhere

"Connie, you're well acquainted with Christ's parable of the ninety-nine sheep, aren't you?"

"Yes."

"Where did Christ leave the ninety-nine sheep when He went to seek the lost one?"

"Safely in the fold, of course."

"Where did He bring the lost one He found?"

"Back to the fold."

"Please open your Bible to Luke 15. I'll read verse 4. 'What man of you, having an hundred sheep, if he lose one of them, doth not leave the ninety and nine *in the wilderness*, and go after that which is lost, until he find it.' And verse 6 says He brought the lost sheep home rather than placing it with the ninety-nine in the wilderness. Do you not see that the ninety-nine are not in as secure a position as we have always thought? They aren't in the fold. In the wilderness, they feel no need to repent. 'There is more joy in heaven over one sinner that repents, than over the ninety and nine who suppose they need no repentance' [Review and Herald, 16 July 1895]. Even Christ had to separate the sinner who repents from those who choose to remain in the wilderness. Do you not see that God is calling for separation?"

A few days later, after much struggling and tears, Connie and her sister consented to leave the Seventh-day Adventist Church and be baptized into "God's final remnant." But Connie's husband refused to accept our message.

We parked our motor homes in an unplanted field while we visited the rest of the church members. The next day, a police officer knocked on our door.

"If I were you, I wouldn't stay here," he warned. "We can't

DARK LIGHT

guarantee your safety out here in the middle of nowhere."

"Thank you for telling us," I said, "but I'm sure we'll be all right." I had faith to believe God would protect His children.

Several nights later, at two in the morning, I awakened to the sound of voices outside our motor home.

Terrified, I could do nothing against so many. Instantly this thought came. *If I weren't so independent, I'd listen to those who know. Have I substituted presumption for faith?*

Trembling, I fell to my knees as a rock hit our roof. Several drunk men just outside our window cursed and yelled horrible threats.

"O God save us," I pleaded. "Hear our cry for help, and forgive me for not listening to the warning."

Just at that moment, I heard the roar of a truck coming down the dirt road. Within seconds, the gang disappeared. The vehicle circled our motor homes and then left. In silence I sat by the window, seeing nothing but the stars.

Questions pounded my brain. Again God had shown His love, even when I refused to listen. *Are His blessings an evidence of His goodness and mercy, in spite of my determination to go my own way? Or is this His way of showing His guidance and approval of what I am doing? Have I misunderstood God's messages and listened to another voice?*

The next morning, we reported the incident at the police station. "You're mighty lucky," the police officer commented. "You could have been hurt or killed. How long will you be here?"

"Almost two months."

"If you wish, you may stay in the parking area right behind our office while you're here." I thanked him.

We visited the members whenever possible, but we had free time for personal study. Impressed by reading the Song of Solomon, we discovered love, a new truth to us.

"Sharon, God's unconditional love contrasts sharply with our harsh feeling toward those who won't accept our message. Somehow I have overlooked Jesus' words, 'Neither do I condemn you.' Have I sinned in lacking mercy toward those who don't agree with us?"

That day, we received a letter from friends in our movement informing us that a doctor we had known in California had left his wife, children, and practice to join our group in the northwest. Our friends ended the letter this way: "Other homes are on the verge of breaking up. We see Jesus' words fulfilled, 'A man's foes shall be they of his own household. . . . He that taketh not his cross, and followeth after me, is not worthy of me' (Matthew 10:36-38). I thought of Connie's situation. Her husband had refused to join with us. Would her home also split up?

As I contemplated this thought, Paul's counsel in 1 Corinthians 7 came instantly to my mind: "If any brother hath a wife that believeth not, and she be pleased to dwell with him, let him not put her away," and "The unbelieving wife is sanctified by the husband" (verses 12, 14).

Was the Bible contradicting itself? Was there no way to harmonize this apparent dichotomy? Had we taken one text to the extreme and forgotten that in God's Word there is balance?

Horror overwhelmed me. What had I done? For the past year and a half, I'd destroyed the unity in many

Adventist churches and families, certain that God had approved. But I didn't love those people. The Shannon church members were my beloved family. I hurt when they hurt, cried when they cried, rejoiced with them when they rejoiced. When I chose to return to Ireland, I thought that I was bringing the gospel of victory and freedom from sin. Instead, I'd split the church, caused heartache and misunderstanding to those I love, and now I might even ruin the home of my good friend.

Like Saul of Tarsus, I had spent all my energy to salvage souls from the false church. Suddenly, I realized that I might be in error–just as Saul had been. Was I wrong in proclaiming that our movement was the last church? Earlier, the Seventh-day Adventist Church had been a boundary that had helped keep me in check. But when I'd cast the church aside as Babylon, I had total freedom to decide truth for myself. Was our message correct, or were there subtle errors I couldn't see? Totally confused, I made a long-distance call to the U.S.

Gary listened while I explained our dilemma and suggested a meeting to rethink our methods, our doctrines, and even the validity of our church. When I had finished, there was silence. Then he spoke slowly but with authority.

"John, you have not learned the lesson of complete submission. To work together, we must see eye to eye. I can't turn back from what God has clearly shown me. To return to Babylon by yielding up the message God has given me would mean my death. Please reconsider–or a gulf will open between us. We will call a meeting, but be sure we cannot go back into confusion. We cannot lie with a harlot; neither can we take her name."

He paused, then added, "Call me when you arrive in the States." And I heard the phone click.

Each step back to the motor home felt as if my feet were made of lead. When Sharon returned, I called our group together. After prayer, I shared my thoughts.

"We've interpreted God's command for Israel to remain separate from the Canaanites as our commission to separate from the Seventh-day Adventist Church. Our method has been this: Explain our message of total freedom from sin. Urge that now is the day of salvation. Insist that the listener, through faith in Jesus, make a decision immediately. If any hesitate or refuse, shake the dust off our feet and go on.

"Consequently, some have cut off relationships with parents, siblings, even husband or wife. If anyone dares to disagree with the leaders or voice another opinion, we condemn them as being void of the Spirit. However, the past few weeks, I have seen a merciful God of infinite pity and love. I fear our methods are harsh, wrong, and not from God."

Tearfully, Sharon asked, "The Shannon church is already split in confusion and turmoil. The damage is done. What can we do to salvage the disaster we created?"

"We will have to go to them, confess our errors, and ask God to heal the hurts we've caused."

Neither Sharon nor I could sleep or eat much the next few days. Our mental anguish and regrets pressed upon us like iron bands, crushing our spirits. Only God could

undo our wrongs and forgive. But could we have gone wrong? How could we have been so sure we were doing God's will? Where was our mistake?

That Sabbath, I spoke to our little Shannon church. Looking at the sad faces in our group, I struggled to keep back my tears. "Dear friends, we have made a terrible mistake. The message we brought you is wrong. I cannot explain our errors, for I don't understand myself. I, too, am confused. But this I do know. Our movement is not God's remnant church. We have sinned against God and you, and we beg of you to forgive us. Please go back to where you first saw the light, the Seventh-day Adventist Church. Ask God to heal the hurts we have caused, and pray for unity and love." For a few moments, I couldn't speak. Then I choked out my plea. "I beg you to please pray for us that we, too, can find our way back to God's truth."

A few weeks later, the five founders of our movement met together with many of the members from the northwest. Having been separated from the group for several months, I was able to notice, for the first time, the emphasis on mind control. No one admitted he or she had a problem. I sensed a façade when they stated that Christians never talk doubt but only faith, so have no problems. Weren't their lives like mine–a mess? I wondered at the front everyone put up. It wasn't real. Yet no one dared to disagree. They used the Bible and Ellen White to prove the validity of their experiences. I felt uncomfortable when I heard the command that all must think and act in

We Belong Nowhere

unity or be under suspicion and condemnation. Alarmed, I recognized the strong group mentality.

When I voiced my disagreements and pleaded that we change our methods, Gary said, "John, God has opened His hand to our church. Many souls are being baptized. More churches are on line now than ever. I had wanted you to be part of it–on the front row. But you cannot help us, having taken the direction you have. I am crying inside. I wanted you with us. But I am disappointed. My hopes may never be realized."

After the meeting, Kevin, Bob, Rick, and I, four of the five original leaders, decided we must leave this offshoot movement that had evolved into a full-blown cult. Almost half of the members left too.

As we returned to our motor home, I turned to Sharon in bewilderment. "We've burned all our bridges and cut ourselves off from all means of support. I have no desire to join any other independent ministry. We're no longer members of the Seventh-day Adventist Church. We belong nowhere. Where shall we go?"

I Will Make Darkness Light

Leaving headquarters, we stopped at the first rest area. While Traci played, we sat on a nearby bench, numb with agony.

Sharon spoke first. "I feel dead inside. All is dark, and my mind whirls in confused circles. Only one thing is clear: God won't forsake us, because He still loves us." She began to cry.

I put my arm around her and drew her close. "I read once that error collapses on itself. But it isn't seen as error until it collapses. I think we have an idea how the disciples felt when all their hope seemed blasted as they watched Christ die."

"John, we studied and prayed constantly. Could we have erred in lining up all the Bible and Spirit of Prophecy statements to say what we wanted them to say? Maybe our zeal blinded us and closed our minds. Maybe the Bible and Ellen White didn't teach the truths we thought they did."

We sat in miserable silence.

"One thing I'm sure about," I finally continued. "Though we've made some terrible mistakes, we've always been God's children. His mercy and compassion won't cast off misguided sinners like us. Maybe the promise in Isaiah 42:16 fits us. 'I will bring the blind by a way they did not know; I will lead them in paths they have not known. I will make darkness light before them, and crooked places straight. These things I will do for them, and not forsake them' [NKJV]."

I saw a faint smile on Sharon's face. "I like that, John. It gives me a ray of hope. He's been with us all along, even in our blindness. He'll guide us from our error into truth."

"Yes, dear, someday we'll understand where we went wrong. But now we need money to live. Where shall we go to find work?"

"I want to leave this area where we're so well known."

"Let's go back to Seattle. I'm sure we have enough gas money to travel that far," I suggested.

We both found jobs bagging groceries at a Safeway in the Seattle area. We didn't make much, but enough to get by. We'd worked several weeks when I saw a runaway cart heading for a car in the parking lot. I dove for it, tripped, and fell. Sharp pains from my ankle let me know that I needed a doctor.

"Where do we go now?" I asked Sharon. "I can't carry groceries on crutches."

"Can you drive to California in an ankle brace?"

"I think so. Maybe Bob would hire me to help as a bricklayer."

By the time we arrived in California, I could hobble around pretty well. But I'd worked just a few days when I

I Will Make Darkness Light

mangled two fingers in the grinding gear of the cement mixer. In spite of bandages and the ankle brace, I kept working. A week later, the scaffolding fell and hit me on the head.

Deeply depressed, I fell into bed that night groaning, "Satan's ruined my self-esteem, messed up my beliefs, stopped my career, and now I get hurt in everything I try."

But my family had to eat, so I couldn't wallow long in self-pity. A friend stopped by. "John, I know of a good-paying job in the Bay Area, but you'll need some training. Yesterday, a tree trimmer fell and broke both his legs, and they're looking for a replacement."

"Nothing to it. My brace comes off tomorrow, and these fingers are getting better. Even though I can't keep upright bagging groceries, probably I'll do OK in a dangerous job like topping trees. Do you think I can safely swing in the treetops managing a chain saw?" We both laughed.

But I did apply and get the job, and soon I became skilled as a tree topper and trimmer. We lived by the side of the road in our motor home–all we could afford.

Several weeks passed. "Sharon, we've been worshiping alone each Sabbath. But I long for Christian fellowship. Even though I don't agree with all its theologians, I'm now convinced that the Adventist Church isn't Babylon. Let's attend this week."

Tears trickled down my cheeks as I felt the awesome joy of being back in God's church again. What a privilege we'd missed.

We approached the pastor after the service. "We'd like to join your church."

DARK LIGHT

"Great!" he said. "But first, please attend the evangelistic meetings now in progress."

"But we've been Adventists all our lives. Must we start all over?" I felt humiliated.

Pride finally yielded. To our surprise, the speaker, Gary Venden, preached the very message of righteousness by faith we'd opposed. In the past, I would always wait after the service to corner the speaker with quotes that would straighten out his theology. But now I had no compelling desire to change him. In fact, I even liked Gary and valued him as a person. I actually preferred him above myself. This was a new experience for me.

After several weeks of meetings, I shared this brand-new feeling with Sharon. "Many times during the meetings, I've disagreed on minor points. Yet I've felt no urge to set him straight, no need to argue. What has happened to my overbearing, dogmatic attitude? I love the freedom and relief of no longer having to convince people of the truth as I see it. Even better, I don't need to help God judge who is saved or lost."

"You, too, John? Jesus has lifted a great burden from me. I feel a genuine love and respect for people, no matter how different their lifestyle or ideas. They're God's children. If He wants to change them, that's His job, not mine."

Sharon and I talked of rebaptism. "I know God has forgiven us. But the hurt and havoc we caused haunt me. I think God would be pleased for us to publicly proclaim that He has buried our guilt and sin and has lifted us to walk in a new life," she said.

Yet hidden deep in our hearts were seeds of stubborn

rebellion we thought were uprooted. It was revealed the evening that the pastor stated firmly, "If you want to join the church, you must be rebaptized."

I bristled inwardly–no one would force me. Immediately, a quotation from *Evangelism* about not insisting on rebaptism popped into my mind. I'd object. Show him he was wrong. Insist on profession of faith. But before I made my case, the evangelist joined us. "No, if John and Sharon don't want to, they must not be forced into rebaptism." The pastor still insisted.

Just as I was ready to lash out with my usual soft-spoken dogmatism, the Lord spoke to my heart. "No, John, you need rebaptism. Look at your spirit. Your resistance! Your independence! You've always fought authority and pushed your own way with an Ellen White quote to back you up. You've never submitted before."

Sharon came to the same conclusion. When the pastor and evangelist left, she said, "John, we do need to be rebaptized."

Traci joined us in baptism. The three of us had the joy of starting again as we were baptized in a little church in central California. How we rejoiced in the freedom Jesus gave us. Self was dying in the joy of preferring others above ourselves. We no longer felt compelled to condemn, even when we saw inconsistencies in the church. Instead of criticizing, we prayed for our new brothers and sisters.

We were hungry, almost starving, for fellowship. If only we could be truly accepted, part of God's family. A friendly couple came to us after church one Sabbath. We felt their warmth and love and were thrilled when they invited,

"Won't you come to our home for lunch next Sabbath?"

What joy! Someone had accepted us. All week, we looked forward to this Christian fellowship. What a privilege to be invited to a church member's home! We could hardly wait. We could belong again. But between Sabbath School and church, my heart skipped a beat as I saw the man come over to us. He leaned over the pew and whispered, "This week, we learned that you are a former offshoot leader. We heard of the havoc you've caused in many homes. I cannot put my family at risk. We can't have you over to our home for lunch. I'm sorry."

We were devastated, rejected. I felt like scum. If only I could crawl out of the church and leave. Neither Sharon nor I heard a thing the minister said. That afternoon, we searched our hearts in sadness.

"This is unbelievable! How could Christians treat us like poison?" Sharon exclaimed.

Then it dawned on me. "Sharon, this is just what we did again and again. This is how we rejected anyone who chose to remain in the church. Remember how we warned everyone that they would be contaminated if they stayed in the Adventist Church? We didn't care about their feelings. Our selfish zeal for God lacked compassion. God had to show us who we were and what we were like. Self-revelation is painful. Like Peter, we can only learn the hard way—through experience. Jesus accepts us, but it'll take longer before people trust us.

"This experience will help us better understand the meaning of Paul's admonition to forbear one another in love [Ephesians 4:2]."

Discovered: Two Sides of Truth

When the tree-service business in the Bay Area sold out, we started our own business near Sharon's parents in northeast Washington. There the local pastor, Leroy Moore, visited us. We opened our hearts to him and told him our story. He saw our repentance, our bewilderment, and our confusion. He must have felt drawn to us, desiring to help untangle us from the blind theological web we had spun.

Putting his hand on my shoulder, he assured me, "John, you may not be aware of the guidance of the Holy Spirit, but you've been unconsciously making progress. I can see that you're now ready to listen, to unlearn, and to relearn. Through pain and humiliation, God has directed you into a different kind of thinking."

A few days later, Pastor Moore came to us with a stack

of papers in a folder. "I've heard that you've done some writing, John. I need your help. I'm in the process of writing a book. Would you two be willing to proofread my manuscript? You'll find typos and duplications. Maybe some parts lack clarity. I'm sure you will be interested in the contents too. I'd really appreciate your input."

"We'd be honored to help in any way we can," I answered.

That evening, with pencil in hand to make corrections, I began reading. I'd not read long when my heart began to pound. "Sharon, come here," I called. "I think I'm beginning to understand. God must have led Elder Moore to write this manuscript for us to help dispel our crooked thinking. He talks about dialectical reasoning."

"So what? Never heard of it." Sharon sounded bored.

"Well, you and I have been using it for years."

"We have? What is it?"

"A one-sided way of thinking. You know how logical I am. But when I discuss truth, it's only from my opinion. I'm almost blind to any other idea."

Sharon smiled. "How well I know! Seems I've lost every argument we ever had. So what does Elder Moore's manuscript have to do with this?"

"He suggests that spiritual truth can be understood only by paradoxical reasoning."

"He uses too many big words. Are we going to have to look up everything in the dictionary?" Sharon objected.

"I'll save you the effort this time. You know that a paradox is a statement that seems self-contradictory, but in reality it expresses a complete truth. Want an example?"

Discovered: Two Sides of Truth

"Might help me understand."

Now that I had Sharon's attention, I continued, "Remember how uncomfortable we felt in separating from the church until I discovered a quotation that seemed to support our plan?" I recited the familiar quotation: " 'hoped that there would not be the necessity for another coming out.' When we were uncertain about what to do at the beginning of another coming out, we felt positive that God provided us with encouragement to let us know we were on track. But we ignored another warning that could have kept us in balance. The same author said, 'When anyone is drawing apart from the organized body of God's commandment keeping people . . . then you may know that God is not leading him. He is on the wrong track' [*Selected Messages*, 3:18]."

"Wow!" Sharon exclaimed. "Exactly the opposite counsel. How could we have harmonized that dichotomy?"

"If only we had been willing to combine both truths, asking for God's balanced counsel, we might have saved ourselves much sorrow. But at the time, our minds were closed."

I continued, "Elder Moore points out that Jesus continually had to combat this wrong method of thinking. Even Christ's closest friends, the disciples, perceived only part of the truth. They saw only the Conquering King prophesies. Their self-centered ambition blinded them to the prophesies depicting the Suffering Lamb. That pretty well describes what happened to us and to others who form an offshoot movement. Now it's plain to me that our one-sided thinking, combined with pride

of opinion, blinded us."

"But, John, why couldn't we see the other side? You remember that pastors from North Carolina to Ireland urged us to consider their point of view."

"I guess that I always had a ready answer for everything someone might throw at me. I knew it already. What someone else considered balance, I mistook for compromise."

"But we were sincere in believing that the faith of Jesus was the hand all-powerful that would give us complete victory over sin."

"Sincere, Sharon, but sincerely wrong in ignoring the other side of truth. We never stressed God's infinite pity, mercy, and forgiveness when we fall. Notice this gem I found this morning: 'To go forward without stumbling, we must have the assurance that a hand all-powerful will hold us up, and an infinite pity be exercised toward us if we fall' [*Signs of the Times*, 28 July 1881].

"I'm ashamed to admit how self-confidence and pride blinded us. Jesus tried over and over to explain the truth of His mission to the disciples, but they couldn't see it either. He had to wait until the crucifixion, when everything fell apart for them, before they could understand. Then He said, 'O fools, and slow of heart to believe all that the prophets have spoken.' Did you notice the word *all?*"

"Yes, I did. So that's where we went wrong. We took only part of God's precious truth, not all of it. Go on; this is beginning to clarify our dilemma."

"Remember this sentence, 'Your only safety is in coming to Christ, and ceasing from sin this very moment' [*Signs of the Times*, 29 August 1892]? We used that statement like a hammer to pound our 'truth' into people, trying to convince them they could immediately become completely sinless. In fact, the context of this statement stresses the urgency of preparing for Jesus' coming. If only we'd balanced it with this concept: 'Day by day the mists of selfishness and sin that envelop the soul are dispelled by the bright beams of the Sun of Righteousness' [*Patriarchs and Prophets*, 134]. That phrase 'dispelling sin day by day' could have brought peace to our friends in Ireland instead of throwing them into despair and confusion."

Just then, Traci came into the room. "Daddy, I don't understand what you are telling Mom. Explain to me in simple words so I'll know what Jesus wants me to do. If I'm supposed to stop sinning this very moment, then why do I still need Him day by day?"

I took my little girl on my knee. "Honey, at first, these two thoughts seem to disagree. But if we think awhile, we can see they fit together perfectly, like two pieces in a jigsaw puzzle."

"You'd better help me think, Daddy. I don't understand."

"You and Jesus are friends. You want to please Him, so you decide to do what He asks. Right?" Traci nodded her head.

"Because you love Him, you want to keep His commandments, which is the same as to stop sinning. So you make a decision right now. You say, 'Jesus, by Your power, I choose not to sin.' Do you agree?"

"Sure, Daddy, but sometimes I do bad things anyway." Traci looked down at the floor.

DARK LIGHT

"I can see you understand that it's not easy to stop sinning. It takes time and prayer and sometimes hard experiences to see how really bad we are inside. Jesus tried to tell Peter the sin of his character, but Peter couldn't see it. Sometimes a fall is what it takes to finally open our eyes to the sins of our character."

"You mean we learn a little at a time—like when I learned the multiplication tables? I couldn't learn them all at once. Just the threes first and the fours later."

"Right. But now that you've learned them all, you can mix them up or put them all together. It's the same with 'stop sinning this very moment' and 'dispelling sin day by day.' You say, 'Jesus, I want to grow like You today and quit sinning now, but please keep pointing out my sins each day so I can ask You for victory.' Do you see how both fit together to help you become like Jesus?"

"I like that, Daddy. Jesus helps me to hate sin so much that I want to stop now, but I need to ask Him every day. He does this over and over again for me."

I hugged her. "That's beautiful, honey. To think it took me seventeen years to figure that out. Can you see that it becomes complete truth when both sides are blended together?"

She nodded her head.

"Remember the battery under the hood of our car?"

"Yes. You showed me there were two poles, a positive and a negative."

"Right. So which pole on our car battery do you prefer to use in getting our car started?" I asked her.

"Both of them. You said that nothing works until both

poles are connected."

"You're a good mechanic." I smiled at her. "And that's the way with truth; we must connect both sides."

Day after day, Sharon and I studied the concepts in Pastor Moore's manuscript. Each day, we discovered areas where we had overstressed one truth and omitted another.

"You'll appreciate this illustration, Sharon. We've used this negative quote to prove that the Adventist Church had become Babylon. Unfortunately, independent groups like ours use this passage to prove that we must separate from and shun all Adventists." I read this familiar passage to her. " 'There is a little hope in one direction: Take the young men and women, and place them where they will come as little in contact with our churches as possible, that the low grade of piety which is current in this day shall not leaven their ideas of what it means to be a Christian' [*Manuscript Releases*, 12:995].

"Now here's the contrasting positive pole for that 'little hope' quotation. 'No advice or sanction is given in the Word of God to those who believe the third angel's message to lead them to suppose that they can draw apart. This you may settle with yourselves forever' [*Selected Messages*, 3:21]."

"Wow! There's pretty heavy tension between those two poles of truth," Sharon commented.

"Sure is. On the one hand, we have the possible need for separation. On the other hand, we are told to settle forever the idea that there will be no drawing apart. Now I see that this tension is needed to bring balance. First, it prevents us from developing a blind confidence in a church organization. At the same time, it will keep us from jumping ship just because certain items on board are not in order."

"Each day, I see more clearly where we went wrong, John. In our zealous sincerity, we longed to be that 'one in twenty' that would be saved. Knowing that the majority would be lost, we wasted no time on them. First, we came down hard on just one side of truth. Next, we reinforced that side so strongly that the neglected truths crumbled. No wonder we grew harsh. Our message lacked love, peace, and compassion–the truth of the full gospel."

"Clinging to only one side of the truth always brings imbalance. We independent folk are not the only ones in trouble."

Sharon looked at me with a question mark on her face. "What do you mean, John?"

"Just this. I can see a danger of deception even for those in the true church. Loyal Adventists can ignore one side of the truth, or diminish it, and lose their spiritual balance too. Our only safety is to believe and accept both poles as true."

Sharon sighed. "If only we'd considered both sides, we wouldn't have detoured into such extreme views."

A few days later, while Sharon was kneading bread in the kitchen, I began to chuckle.

"What's so funny about Moore's manuscript?" she asked, coming to the door of my study.

"Can you take a minute?"

"Sure. Let me wash my hands."

Discovered: Two Sides of Truth

"Moore has a unique illustration of how our thinking can blind us to something that is quite obvious to someone else. Read this sentence only once."

FINISHED FILES ARE THE RE-
SULT OF YEARS OF SCIENTIF-
IC STUDY COMBINED WITH
THE EXPERIENCE OF YEARS.

"Now count the *F*s in that square. Count them only once. Don't go back and recount them."

Sharon did as I directed.

"How many *F*s did you find?" I asked her.

"Three."

I began to laugh again. "Must be why we make a team—we're both blind. That's all I found the first time too. Most of us see only half of the *F*s. But there are six; only our method of reading allows us to skip all the *F*s in the three *of*s."

"And that kind of blindness led us right out of the church." Sharon put her hand on my shoulder. "I see how we drifted farther and farther from truth. We compiled a certain category of quotations and focused on them alone, totally ignoring those that could have brought balance. That's why we sincerely believed God called us to separate from our former brothers and sisters."

"Maybe our journey into and out of fanaticism can yet be a blessing. Though I've written many letters asking forgiveness, I know that many people will never come back." Again I felt overwhelmed with a feeling of horror and re-

gret at what I'd done.

"I pray that God can use me to help others when they get off the track. I'll counsel them to do what the disciples did. They went back to the upper room, the last place where they met Jesus. Then He came to them with the message 'Peace be unto you.' As He did with the disciples on the road to Emmaus, He'll open *all* Scripture to them."

"But it takes so long to overcome blindness of the mind, especially when we're so sure we're right and are so proud of our opinions." Sharon sighed with regret.

"I know. It's hard to understand the folly of stressing negative statements or separating them from other truths like we did. My desire in life is to prevent that blindness by pointing out the beautiful balance and hope that fill both the Bible and the Spirit of Prophecy. I pray daily that God will help me to blend truth the way Jesus did."

I saw tears of joy filling Sharon's eyes. "John dear, our prayers are being answered. No longer do I feel cut off from God when I make a mistake. If I'm not rebellious, I know His righteous love will forgive and cover me. I thank God for the assurance that I'm accepted through the blood of Jesus."

I took her in my arms and hugged her. "Sweetheart, I'm thrilled at how the Holy Spirit is guiding us into *all* truth. He's healing our blindness."

"John, like Isaiah's promise, He's opening our blind eyes. He's humbled our pride. These new paths have led us from darkness into light. Beautiful truths we didn't know or understand are straightening out our crooked paths."

With bowed heads, we whispered together, "Thank You, God, for not forsaking us."

CHAPTER FIFTEEN

Epilogue

Not only did John and Sharon Witcombe keep on studying to find spiritual truth, but they also determined to prepare themselves for further service for God. So they returned to school to finish their education.

During the time they studied at the university, John took many speaking appointments in surrounding churches. Not only did he share how God led him back to truth and balance, but he urged the church members to live the light God has given them. He stresses, "If we just love one another, preferring those with whom we differ above ourselves, no matter whether they are to the right or to the left of where we currently are, there might be less problem with separation movements. Come to think of it, if we truly loved one another, we probably wouldn't still be here on this earth."

DARK LIGHT

When John spoke to pastors at a workers' meeting about how to deal with members who are joining independent ministries, he counseled, "If friends of yours leave the church to join an independent movement, do what Jesus did. Wash their feet, rather than debate with them. By your words and actions, show that you still prefer them before yourself. This is practicing the reality of what foot-washing symbolizes."

Both John and Sharon graduated with honors from Eastern Washington University with bachelor of science degrees in community-health education. John also received the student-of-the-year award.

Currently, John, Sharon, and Traci live in Spokane, Washington, where John pastors both the Spokane Countryside and the Davenport Seventh-day Adventist Churches.

Pastor Leroy Moore's manuscript that the Witcombes worked on was published by the Review and Herald Publishing Association in 1995 under the title *Adventism in Conflict.* John and Sharon believe the information in *Adventism in Conflict* to be an invaluable supplement for those who have read this book.